Praise

Clear, funny, huma
internet brings ou
but Cross might be
razor-sharp logic and empathetic vision, she
guides us away from posing and posting toward
the work of building a better world.

—Jude Ellison S. Doyle, author of Dead Blondes & Bad Mothers and Trainwreck

Katherine Cross innately understands both what's so alluring about social media and what's so dangerous about it. Instead of writing a polemic, however, she's written a book that looks beyond our screens to a whole world whose problems won't be solved through posting. Compassionate, incisive, and funny, *Log Off* might make you (literally) touch grass.

—Emily St. James, author of Monsters of the Week

Serves as a gateway between epochs: a past where the internet still gave hope of collective, grassroots organizing, and a future where we have squandered that potential for a couple cheap laughs and ephemeral popularity. *Log Off* proffers a world where we take digital citizenship as a serious and valuable tool—just one of many in the toolbox — for building a better world. As someone whose posts have changed the world and who is guilty many times over of the sins Katherine describes, I cannot agree more.

—Emily Gorcenski

A fascinating meditation on how social media has falsely seduced the planet into believing that it represents a gigantic step forward for humanity, written by a woman with a lifetime of experience in the extremely online trenches. Despite the title, Cross's book doesn't ask that we all delete our accounts: instead, she's asking for the more radical step of rethinking our relationship to Online.

—Faine Greenwood

Joyous and informative. Simultaneously a collection of standalone essays and a comprehensive whole, *Log Off* sees Katherine Cross explore the politics of social media, the problems those spaces host and create, and what we — collectively, and individually — can do about it. Written with a loving cynicism, *Log Off* leaves the reader with new answers, new questions, and a new sense of hope.

—Os Keyes, University of Washington

Katherine Cross

Why Posting and Politics (Almost) Never Mix

Copyright © 2024 by Katherine Cross
Published by LittlePuss Press LLC
Brooklyn NY
www.LittlePuss.net

LittlePuss

Selections of "It's Not Your Fault You're An Asshole on Social
Media" and "The Oubliette of Terror" previously appeared
in modified form in WIRED magazine.

Cover design by Zach Bokhour
Cover Photo by Billy Huynh
Proof-read by John Sweet
Edited by Cat Fitzpatrick & Casey Plett

Printed and bound in the United States

Library of Congress Cataloging-in-Publication Data is available

ISBN 978-1-7367168-6-1 (print)
ISBN 978-1-7367168-7-8 (e-book)

10 9 8 7 6 5 4 3 2 1

For Rachel
For lighting the long roads of my life.

For Athena
*For keeping me sane with the conversations
that made this book happen.*

For Heather
*Because I promised the woman
I thought you were.*

For Esther
*Because I believe in the woman
you'll become.*

And for everyone who ever wanted
to throw their phone across the room
because of something
they read online.

CONTENTS

Log Off

Introduction

"The end of the world is just a hypothesis." That lyric from *Penguindrum*'s opening theme lived rent-free in my head as I lay sleeplessly staring at my Twitter feed throughout the bleak early nights of the COVID-19 pandemic. Yes, hopeless nerd that I am, I consoled myself with a soothing refrain from an anime song. The words were easy to say, far harder to believe in those long hours and longer days that made up the temporal sludge of 2020.

This was before a *New Yorker* cartoon popularized the word *doomscrolling*, so I didn't quite have a name for this compulsive flipping through terrible news story after terrible news story that I seemed unable to refrain from. As the novel coronavirus spread out from the world's major cities like red ink blots from a leaky pen, I became intimately acquainted with statistics about Italian, Iranian, and Chinese administrative regions. I couldn't sleep, I could barely eat, I wept. But there was one pinprick of light that gave me some hope (perhaps equally hard to believe now, in 2024): public health experts on Twitter.

In the midst of this seeming-apocalypse, these scientists, doctors, scholars, and journalists were performing heroic feats of science communication, opening up a free, limitless-capacity graduate seminar in fields like epidemiology, virology, infectious disease, internal medicine, and more. Twitter's capacity for allowing dorky obsessives to write fifty-tweet-long threads about Romanian stamps from the 1920s, or sixteenth-century Dutch cheese, or lost *Doctor Who* episodes, was being mobilized for the public good. People needed answers yesterday about this deadly new virus and what they could do to protect themselves. Like angels crowned with coruscating halos made of the Matrix itself, these experts moved among us, offering the best advice they could on how to interpret the barrage of new stats we were receiving (we became newly minted experts in what *R-nought* meant!), and how to practise pandemic-era hygiene.

Even better? Some of these experts were calling for radical reorganizations of society, for seizing the moment to finally realize long-held dreams that had been deferred by artificial political gridlock and transnational capitalism.

If ever there was a moment that tested the ability of social media to take the lead in changing the world, in organizing and mobilizing us to press for lasting, structural change, COVID was it. Had this pandemic happened in 1990, we'd have been stuck indoors sending letters and using MCI long-distance to stay connected to our loved ones and communities. But now? Now we had the world in our pockets — instant communication, HD video, crowdsourcing, and the thoughts of millions streaming through our consciousness at any given moment. Because COVID happened in 2020, we at least had the tools to get around the loss of in-person contact, and could redouble our efforts to change the world.

Or so it seemed.

Then it all became Extremely Online.

***

By the time we reached our strange pandemic summer, fissures were already beginning to form, with some experts maintaining the need for the strictest possible interventions, like long-term lockdowns, while others began to advocate for a "harm reduction" approach that would leave parts of society open. Advice became contradictory — don't mask, then mask up; parks should be open, no they should be closed — and their priors became more ideological, with libertarian-leaning scientists proving more sceptical of government intervention, as for instance with the so-called "Great Barrington Declaration".

Meanwhile, the public was growing unhappy with the slow and furtive pace of scientific investigation. Is it safe to send my kids to school or not? Can I go to my grandmother's funeral or not? People wanted The Truth, and science had to remind them that research could only provide partial answers at the best of times. And who in the name of the Goddess and Her Consort could've mistaken these for the best of times?

It wasn't long before the experts began openly bickering. Among their fandoms, things were worse still: complex theories and analysis were reduced to slogans like "wear a fucking mask!" or "back to normal" or "vaxxed and relaxed." Experts themselves became subject to virulent threats against their lives, livelihoods, and families, especially if they were women. Some medical experts I knew personally began retreating from Twitter or quitting it altogether due to harassment — not just from right-wing extremists, who by now were breathing massive new life into the anti-vax movement, but from their own colleagues who considered them either too lax or too strict in the advice they gave.

In every case, the once-broad horizon of building a better world on the ashes of the pandemic was narrowed to a blazing pinhole of individual, politically charged actions. We asked how to change the world and got told how to best protect ourselves and little else. Twitter's structural individualism had come back to haunt us with a vengeance.

***

I will admit, my faith in social media had already been dwindling even before this. I'd watched its myriad flaws and abuses over the previous decade, from harassment campaigns like GamerGate to explosive privacy violations like the Cambridge Analytica scandal at Facebook. However, I still held out hope that some hashtag campaigns and co-ordinated communication could lead our societies to a better place, *so long as these campaigns succeeded in getting us to do meaningful things in the physical world and not just on our phones or at our desks.*

That turned out to be the sticking point. And in 2020 it was what finally snuffed my last remaining embers of faith in the ability of these platforms to help us achieve noble, collective aims. In a few months we went from "free, universal health care in America now!" to "wear a fucking mask!" and we couldn't even achieve the latter.

Many, of course, advocated for both. But, in addition to the basic physics behind there only being so many hours in a day, social media was a far better conduit for one of these types of demands. Social shaming around individualistic behaviours — even those with a collective benefit, like masking up during COVID surges — is far easier to pull off with the platforms available to us than building the kind of political power necessary to achieve universal health care. Social media quickly reduces any sort of radical aspiration to a slogan, mere signalling, but it can be used very effectively to harangue an individual for their perceived poor choices. It also allows you to endlessly vent your spleen about your grief, fears, and anxieties in order to soothe yourself — and who didn't need that amidst the worst pandemic in over a century? In the process, the ferment for structural change dissipated and all that energy followed the path of least resistance — into the personal and the individualized.

All we succeeded in doing was terrifying the people who listened into a quiescent paralysis that presented them with yet more social media as the only solution to their problems, creating a small cadre of Twitter power users who pored over the details of medical journals they barely understood, steeped in confirmation bias as they sought to prove COVID was either a mislabelled common cold or the Andromeda strain that would leave us all with long COVID within a few years.

The pandemic left me convinced that social media presented us with only an illusion of collective action — we're all online together sharing the same ideas, memes, and hashtags, how could that *not* be collective? — while instead isolating us in our own oubliettes of confirmatory terror. To the extent that Black Lives Matter has found any traction at all, it's precisely to the degree that it sought to make an impact beyond social media, beyond merely "raising awareness." #MeToo, meanwhile, is emerging as a dismal failure precisely because it became little more than a bitter harvest of our deepest traumas, ready to be liked, shared, and quoted — a strip mine of #content.

The whole point was to show our scars as women. We gave *Jezebel* and BuzzFeed some headlines, which fed right back into the social media ecosystem to start the life cycle anew. There were a handful of high-profile victories — who couldn't cheer at the demise of Harvey Weinstein? — but what really changed? Perhaps a few token policies here and there, but nothing that actually protects us. COVID-posting too was quickly reduced to a similar parade of anecdotal traumas and the viral emotions that surrounded them.

∗∗∗

The question I hope to try to answer with this book is, *why*? But also, I want to examine how we, especially among the political left and its constituent movements like feminism, came to believe that the revolution had to be live-tweeted. This myth of social media's indispensability to our movements, not just as a tool but as *the* forum for change, is dangerous. If we internalize it too deeply, it actually *demobilizes* our movements, lulling us into mistaking quote-tweet wars and "clapbacks" for meaningful political action, seducing us into seeing nanoseconds of digital catharsis as an adequate substitute for change. It seduces us into mistaking the profitable content we generate for truly resistive speech — as well as tying our worth and our success, as people and activists, to the engagement metrics created by large tech corporations.

It's old hat by now to say that social media is problematic or that tech is political. Technological historian Langdon Winner argued "certain

17

technologies in themselves have political proper-
ties" in 1980, before I was born. But I want to mod-
ify this argument a little bit. I don't want to tell
you that screen time is bad for your kids or that
social media is rotting your attention span; I don't
even want to focus too much on the social problems of online harassment and disinformation.
Instead, I put to you the following: the idea that
tech is political sometimes obscures the ways in
which social media may be *anti-political.*

You may be sceptical of such a claim. Social media
is chock-a-block with political content, hashtag
activism, and disinformation that turns grand-
parents into fascists. How could it be *anti*-
political?

Because it demobilizes and scatters the polity;
it makes it much harder to come together, deliberate, and effect change in our communities.
Worse, social media tricks us into thinking that
that's *exactly* what we're doing. What results is
a "public square" where real people can get hurt
but nothing ever really changes. If social media
has power to do good, it lies in its ability to *act*
as a conduit between different domains of the
physical world — in other words, how it can help
you act in your community. Where it's failed us
most dramatically, however, is that it has become
predominantly self-referential, keeping us stuck
on platforms obsessing over things that only
really matter *there* — a problem made worse when
internet drama is dressed in the stolen valour of
genuinely weighty political issues.

This all matters for a few reasons. First and foremost, one of the ugliest side effects of terminal COVID-posting that proliferated amongst the Extremely Online was a deepening mistrust of their fellow human being; every time they fell for outrage-bait about some wanker being a dick about not wearing a mask, their inevitable response was, "I don't trust people anymore!" This is a neat fit for conservatives, whose entire movement is built on a notion of Original Sin, developed through two centuries of monarchism, fascism, nativism, and lesser varieties of know-nothingism, that treats strangers as essentially threats. But for anyone to the left of Mussolini, such contempt for your fellow human being, such unwillingness to reach out to one's neighbour for fear they'll be like That Bitch from Panera Bread I Saw on TikTok, is extraordinarily dangerous — and fatal to realizing the ideals we share, which are necessarily collective.

Secondly, speaking of TikTok, which may already be banned in parts of the US by the time this book reaches your hands/screen, I am finding myself watching history repeat itself. If you're in your early twenties, you may be too young to remember former vice president Al Gore, among others, waxing poetic about how platforms like Twitter were going to change the world because of protests in Iran in the late aughts, or how the Colour Revolutions that proliferated across Eastern Europe — which continue to haunt the dreams of autocrats across

Eurasia — showed that the internet had come of age, creating self-organizing communities that were invincible against the onslaught of sclerotic state actors and tyrants.

Twitter was often cast as indispensable to these movements. The Arab Spring, and all its attendant Twitter use, represented the culmination of this mythology, but protests in Greece against the EU's immiseration of that country, the occupation of Istanbul's Gezi Park, and Occupy Wall Street were other high-water marks. Twitter seemed to be the secret sauce.

Yet where are we now, exactly, in the wake of all that? Ukraine's democratic project was given new life not by hashtags but by a war for its very survival. Elsewhere, the hard, slow, grinding work of politics continues, long after local protest movements ceased to appear on the "trending" pane of Twitter.

TikTok has taken over the role that Twitter once had as the supposed agent of change. What Twitter was for millennials like myself, TikTok is for GenZ: synonymous with the generation of youth who will single-handedly save us all from the coming car crash of apocalypses. Consider this a warning from a girl born in 1986 who's watched this cycle play out after being flattered, scapegoated, and forgotten by her elders: TikTok will not change the world in the way you hope. It is a trap to pretend it will. The proposed US TikTok ban is both a catastrophic intrusion on free expression and totally idiotic, but some arguments being made against it — namely, the idea that the progressive movement can't live without Tik-Tok — are steeped in a mythology of social media indispensability that has already turned the last decade into sociological wreckage. I hope to use this little book to challenge the myth that we need these platforms more than they need us. After all, Twitter was supposed to be a change agent, and look at it now.

Don't blame Elon Musk, either. He's merely Twitter's all too Dantean punishment: an Extremely Online man who became so addicted to the platform that he spent US$44 billion buying it just to post ten-year-old memes without the risk of getting banned for irredeemable cringe — and so that he could roll back Twitter's already threadbare policies protecting trans people. This Most Divorced Man in the Universe is, in many ways, the avatar of everything Twitter is: nasty, churlish, obsessive, abusive, prejudicial. But the site was already in steep decline when he bought it, already a shell of its former self that had become known as the Hellsite even to those who remained hopelessly in its thrall. If you think Twitter is for old people, then I hope to tell you some of the story of how it got old. But if you don't, then I hope to show you why Twitter has aged poorly and why you should do as the title says.

***

Speaking of, let's talk about the title.

21

When the idea for this book was batted around between me and my editors, one of the possible title concepts was "Delete Your Account." But I stuck with my original idea of "Log Off" because, as one of the hopelessly online people I'll be talking about in this book, I'm sensitive to the contextual differences between the two phrases. "Delete your account" means to fuck off into the sun, disintegrating your platform presence with it. "Log off" *can* mean this, but other times it's a form of tough love. Or even regular ol' love. It can be a way of telling someone they're being Too Online and need to step away.

"Touch Grass" conveys the same sentiment and was another title idea. But that phrase is usually hurled as invective at someone who is obsessively fixated on internet drama, like Jesse Singal or half the columnists at the *New York Times*. "Log Off" can be a loving plea as well as invective. It can be a way of saying, delicately, that there is some grass in your area desperately in need of touching without actually *shouting* that at you. And that, in the end, is what the title means: You don't need to give up social media. You just need to use *it* rather than letting it use *you*. Sometimes that means finding other tools for the jobs you need to do.

I do not intend to be an old woman shouting at clouds, but as both a scholar and a poster, I've learned the hard way that there are limits to what these platforms can do. That does not mean they have no utility whatsoever. There are some things that social media can do very well, and that it should be used for; there are positive possibilities for what the internet *can* look like if we get over the myth of social media's indispensability. You can reduce the harm to yourself and others by stepping back a bit, using social media less, and using it for fewer purposes than you once did without completely deleting your web presence. Information technology is here to stay. We need to be involved and engaged with it to shape it for the betterment of humanity. Primitivist fantasies merely cater to the gaggle of libertarian "disruptors" who already wield far too much power in Silicon Valley.

But the worst people in the Valley also thrive on all the demobilizing disengagement that their platforms have slowly led us towards. They have alchemized activism into toxic Twitter beefs and seduced us into thinking that we're one viral campaign away from solving some massive socio-structural problem, which makes it all the easier to devote our energies to pursuing these digital white whales in lieu of more tangible goals in our lives and communities. The self-soothing they offer, free at the point of delivery, actually comes at a great cost to our ability to see ourselves as real political actors — a cost I see every day when I see someone (often people who should know better) doomposting about how there's no hope for humanity,

We're not condemned to this. You probably sense it in your own life every time you look up from your phone or step away from the computer: the sense that the world you see through the scroll of Twitter or TikTok or Instagram isn't the world you see when you step away. Sometimes for the worse, but often for the better. On Twitter, it's Apocalypse Forever; in your life, the apocalypse competes for purchase with all that is good and wonderful in your life. Staying in touch with that reality is what's going to prepare you for challenges we face — and those that await us.

One of the things I really can't forgive social media for is how deeply it has corroded our sense of sincerity, making it uncool to care. Yes, it's allowed us to treat everything in our lives like an episode of *Mystery Science Theater 3000*, because it often deserves it. My graduate school cohort has a Slack where we backchannel and make memes about the vicissitudes of grad student life because it's fun, funny, and a release valve. But then I think of my work as a teacher, which reminds me that "citizenship" means something far more than describing what passport you hold. It means that you're part of a community, with duties and obligations towards your neighbours, as well as inherently possessed of rights and dignity for yourself. One of the most grievous sins of anti-immigration discourse in Western countries is how deeply it buries this understanding. Over the next few chapters, I hope to help you see the value in that dignity — and how social media is so often beneath yours.

Social media acts as a self-organizing collective that foments citizenship far less often than it *denies* it to you — making you something less than what you are, spackling over the cracks with a lot of (admittedly sometimes very good) humour. But you don't need to make that trade-off. This, in the end, is something I pray is a hopeful message: by logging off more than you do, you can get the jokes and benefits, *and* you can get the rewards of citizenship.

Logging off is woefully insufficient, but it *is* an essential first step.

***

That said, I understand how much I'm asking here, even if I do mean "log off" in a very limited, time-bounded way. There is an essentially Roach Motel quality to these platforms, what I would describe as *open social media*; it's easy to enter and almost impossible to leave. They're open when you come in, but when you want to go, it turns out they're a *walled garden* instead. Indeed, what these two apparently opposite paradigms turn out to be, it seems to me (and this is a metaphor I'll return to), is a Möbius strip: you carry on far enough along one side of the opposition and suddenly you find yourself on the other.

What makes these platforms "open" is a combination of their ease of access and their ubiquity. Posting is public by default; locking your account or making it less public necessarily cuts you off from many of the platform's greatest benefits, and you're generally speaking to an entire crowd — the entire platform's user base, potentially, rather than merely a curated audience of devoted followers. But the longer you stay, the more you *need* to stay; your friends are there, your career may rely on the platform now. Moving your followers, your networks, your community becomes hard or impossible. The garden suddenly has walls.

It's easy to mummify oneself in lofty justifications for the fulfilment of these basic — but very much real, valid — needs. Politics is the first and best justification for sticking around: you're not just clinging to a platform you've become dependent on, you're making yourself "visible," making your "voice heard," holding malefactors "accountable." As we'll see, this quickly leads to dark places, to a species of online "activism" utterly divorced from any kind of mind-independent reality.

The reason for that is that platforms like Twitter, far from being unique change agents, can only effectively solve problems that they themselves create — and then only those problems that exist primarily on the platform. Call it the unspoken iron law of social media: the more you look at recent history, the more you realize social media has not meaningfully addressed social problems. To the degree it *creates* them, it does so because the problems in question are uniquely well-suited to the way social media points individuals at other individuals. Twitter can facilitate hate speech and hate crimes; it cannot get us to build, say, a community centre. For that, we need real politics: pavement-pounding, letter-writing, town-halling, street-protesting, ballot-casting politics.

But even the splashy, attention-getting street protests of the last decade, not unreasonably attributed to social media's unique crowd-sourcing abilities, are not sufficient, and their decade of failures makes that abundantly clear — with one Spring or Colour Revolution or Occupy movement after another yielding no meaningful change or, worse, far-right governments and dictatorships.[1] Social media has made it all too easy for us to focus on the wrong things, on trivial, private, cathartic non-victories at the expense of things that might last. And it is terrible at *organizing* us in the kind of leadership-driven, hierarchical fashion that would be ideal for channelling masses of people into collective, unitary projects. It is, however, good for cleaning up a few of its own messes.

As we'll see, we haven't been the gainers from that particular trade. Instead, social media has seen us become worse at and more contemptuous of politics, in exchange for the feel-good purism of online humour and a catharsis-driven sense of our own deeply private virtue. These sentiments are many things, but they are not the cornerstones of a community worth living in.

Step One: Log Off of Twitter, or X, or Bluesky, or...

I'm engaged here in an argument I never wanted to make. Believe me, the last thing I'd want to even *appear* to be is an Old who blamed social media for all the world's ills. For me, the internet's benefits were always obvious. I grew up in a small Bronx apartment, in a bedroom with a massive hole in the ceiling that didn't get fixed for years. When I logged on in 2003, a whole universe opened up to me. I was arguing with Brits and Aussies on the *Independent*'s message board about the Iraq War, I was LiveJournaling and making friends in Edmonton, Tokyo, the Philly suburbs, and much, much more. And of course, from 2005, I played *Neverwinter Nights* online as a female character for inexplicable reasons, and anyway, now my name is Katherine and I'm a woman.

I made lifelong friends overseas, explored myself, broke free of the small world I'd always dreamt of escaping every time I clicked on every national capital entry on Encarta '96, staring longingly at those low-res pictures, imagining visiting them all for real one day. There was, and remains, magic to what the internet represented. Social media was just *all that* but faster — and its benefits are undeniable too. There's a strong argument that I'm able to write this book in the first place because social media crowd-sourced enough people to care about my work (including some of you!)

Given my history, surely I could never credibly make a "root of all evil" argument about social media, much less a "Yet you participate in society. Curious!"-style one.[2] And yet, here I am.

***

Twitter's slow-burning collapse, kindled by the (double) lightning bolt of Musk's takeover of the platform and his subsequent drive to turn it into a more thickly populated Gab, prompted widespread discussion of social media, jolting many of us out of the complacent faith that its current form is inevitable and immutable. Some went as far as to doubt the need for social media altogether. Noted Digital Media Studies scholar Ian Bogost, for instance, from the heights of a column in *The Atlantic*, has proclaimed that "the age of social media is ending."[3] Bogost argues: "We cannot make social media good, because it is fundamentally bad, deep in its very structure. All we can do is hope that it withers away, and play our small part in helping abandon it."

Others are less drastic. "Isn't there another way forward?" they wonder. Perhaps even the most strident leftist activist, the most committed hater of Elon Musk and other tech barons, still entertains the secret hope that something like "Twitter But Good, Actually" remains possible, that somewhere out there is a better form of open social media, a Web 2.0 platform with no harassment abuse, disinformation, or extremists. So, of course, voices have arisen that cater to this hope.

In late 2023, for instance, tech journalist Katie Notopoulos took up the banner of federation in *MIT Technology Review* — federation being the idea of decentralizing platforms from vast metropolises into small towns.[4] Something a bit closer to Web 1.0, more blogs, more private websites, smaller forums, and Mastodon-like social media protocols that are divided into "servers" with a high degree of friction between them.

There are excellent reasons for supporting such a move, of course. The most important is data ownership. Much is being made of this by companies like Bluesky, marketing its smooth, Mastodon-like AT Protocol as the "billionaire-proof" future of social media. You'd, in theory, have more control over your data, more ability to curb unwanted virality, the ability to move your networks away from undesirable locations when the next Elon Musk tries to take them over, and, hopefully, less toxicity overall.

Notopoulos concludes with a dose of techno-optimism that's worth quoting in full:

The fix for the internet isn't to shut down Facebook or log off or go outside and touch grass. The solution to the internet is more internet: more apps, more spaces to go, more money sloshing around to fund more good things in more variety, more people engaging thoughtfully in places they like. More utility, more voices, more joy.

Perhaps you can see where I might disagree with this valediction — and, as you read through the rest of this book, you may also see some productive overlap in our arguments. But the big point of divergence is one of faith — faith that the worst *social* aspects of social media can be cleansed through these tools.

Having been on this merry-go-round many times before, I know what techno happy-talk sounds like. I still remember very clearly a 2000 commercial from Nortel Networks. To a cover of the Beatles' "Come Together" a sign loudly asking "What do YOU want the internet to be?" appears all over the planet and a sultry voice-over declares: "More reliable, higher quality, faster, more profitable, Nortel Networks is building a new high-performance internet. And it can be whatever you want it to be." The company didn't even sell products for the average consumer; the ad was selling an *idea* of the internet.[5] Optimistic, forward-looking. (And, of course, it was also selling the white-hot Nortel stock that was just months away from crashing the Canadian stock market.) The ad's an interesting curio, but I could almost *hear* "Come Together" playing as I read Notopoulos's conclusion.

What if we could go back to the internet of that time? If it were possible, it probably would represent an improvement over where we are today. But it's not, actually, a solution and certainly not one that precludes the occasional fondling of grass. I know this because I've actually *been* on Mastodon and Bluesky.

My trans women-led Mastodon server collapsed under a tsunami of drama set off by the transfer of years-old beefs from Tumblr, Twitter, and Reddit — and this was all amidst a surge of new users who'd abandoned Twitter, many of whom were rightly complaining about anti-Black racism on Mastodon when they arrived.

Meanwhile, Bluesky has managed to approximate Twitter far more precisely, in ways good and mostly bad, rapidly adopting all of Twitter's petty hatreds, along with its flair for unnecessary theatrics, exaggerations, distortions, and disinformation. The site remains relatively small, at about four million users as of this writing, but it already groans under the weight of internecine warfare between members of marginalized groups and the soul-destroying leftist infighting for which social media acts as a particle accelerator.

In between the memes are unproductive callouts, character assassinations, cases of terminal irony poisoning, and all the usual Twitter-esque Discourse that we've come to know and hate.

It isn't generational, either: the Zoomers can prove just as toxic as their millennial and Gen X forebears on these platforms.

There is no "Twitter-but-Good-Actually" on the horizon. Even if we have questions about Bogostian techno-pessimism, no techno-optimist *deus ex machina* is going to save us. The problems with social media are not problems with its media, but problems with its sociality. *That* is the hard truth I've had to accept.

***

Through its basic design, Web 2.0 social media subtly structures our online sociality such that the answer to every problem always appears to be more or "better" posting. It does this by combining the apparently contradictory features of an "open platform" and a "walled garden."

What makes a platform "open" is ease of access and ease of virality. Anyone can make an account, and anyone can see your tweets or your Tik-Tok videos, and if you get lucky (or very unlucky), there's nothing stopping your posts from surging wildly in popularity. What makes it a "walled garden," however, is that the point is to keep you there by satisfying what you think is your every emotional, libidinal, even practical need through the platform: friends, hornyposting, crowdfunding, memes, political outrage, personal drama, personal drama stuffed in a turducken *with* memes and political outrage.

This has proven to be especially true with micro-blogging — Twitter and its small army of clones — but it could apply to many other forms of open social media, such as Instagram, whose network effects frequently create the worst of all worlds: an energy-draining illusion of activity that does nothing except make people miserable, exploiting what is often touted as social media's greatest strength but only ever doubling down on its greatest weakness.

This tendency to circularity has particularly worrying consequences for the many left-wing and progressive activists who've come to rely on social media. The problem is not that leftists have too much fun with posting, it's that we are constantly encouraged by the basic design features of the platforms we use to start seeing posting itself as a form of praxis — as not just entertaining, but *virtuous*. This is the logic that leads to people thinking "Let's get [X] trending!" is activism.

But posting is not praxis. Posting *can* be useful on occasion — and it can certainly be hilarious, personally profitable, and even cathartic. But it can't change the world, at least not in the way many might hope.

The delusion that "posting is praxis" appears across a broad political spectrum. It infects self-serious liberals who are convinced that "rational debate" is key to the vital political art of persuasion and who believe social media is the optimal public square in which to make this happen. But it also affects progressives and leftists who might dunk on those Very Serious People at every opportunity, who are themselves kept online by desires for representation, to speak truth to power, to feel seen and to be heard after being excluded, discriminated against, and counted out.

In each case there is the unspoken hope that your posting, whether in the form of argumentation, self-revelation, or even dunking, will somehow move someone you've never met and thereby make the world a better place — if only in pointillist fashion. What makes this hope so hard to resist is that, on occasion, it can seem as though it is justified. These days, I have a fairly visible presence as a trans woman on social media, and before that I was active as a blogger, and before that I spent several strange years as a Reddit mod on r/TwoXChromosomes. In all these incarnations, my visibility has, other trans women have occasionally told me, inspired them to come out themselves.

To hear such accounts of my impact feels good. It's flattering. It's also, at the risk of my sounding a bit cold for a moment, not entirely true. I'm pretty sure I'm not the *main* reason those people came out. I might have been a useful signpost on their journey, and that's a lovely thing to be. But I wasn't indispensable. I changed less than I'd have liked to believe.

I've even, perhaps more strikingly, had someone I knew from Reddit come back to me after years and tell me they'd gone from being an MRA to being a feminist, and that I was the one who helped start them on that journey. Perhaps I did help. But if I did, I was just one small part of a longer journey, which *they made themselves* and didn't necessarily need me for. More importantly, how many other MRAs did I argue with and make no difference to at all? On platforms that thrive on conflict, and where you're more likely to *see* conflict rather than peaceful reconciliation, whether because of algorithms or the summative output of our expressed desires on these platforms, you're not apt to change many minds that weren't already amenable to it.

Instead, what most online activism does is signal membership of an in-group. This is true of Matt Yglesias-style "persuasive" summaries of duelling Substacks, the production and sharing of which serves primarily to demonstrate *bien pensant* status among a particular set of Acela-corridor nuance-mongers, but it is also, alas, true of hashtag activism of the #BelieveWomen variety. Such activity functions primarily not as persuasion but as a way of like-minded people finding each other or wearing the appropriate team colours.

The power of this sort of team-sports group attachment explains why, even now, more than a few people subscribe to the idea that the reason Elon Musk bought Twitter, and why so many of the world's most powerful awful people supported the takeover, was that it represented a conspiracy to silence us nattering radicals and take away our beloved platform. Because Twitter gave them such a powerful feeling of belonging, they make the mistake of thinking that it was ever theirs. And then, of course, that the only way to avenge the loss of the platform is to stay on it, posting harder and harder until... you make Elon Musk cry, I suppose?

***

Which, in point of fact, they did succeed in doing, for a while. I'll concede that, especially in the immediate aftermath of Musk's takeover, the site suddenly became *extremely funny*, funnier than it had ever been, and, most of all, more on-target than it had ever been.

This moment of success in hurting Elon's fee-fees, I want to argue, can function as a useful synecdoche for many arguments in favour of self-referential social media activism. A close examination of it, accordingly, can help make clear not only what actually worked (if only for a time) but also why the big picture still shows a cavalcade of failure that demands we log off from Twitter — permanently.

Twitter was always best at solving problems created by Twitter. Consider how victims of hate websites have been able to network together and fight back against the people who crowdsourced abuse against them. Among the *many* things Musk failed to realize before he took over the site was that he and his every effort on the platform would be carpet-bombed by trolls who'd spent years perfecting their art with these tools.

Log Off

Thus it was that his ill-conceived campaign of revenge against the platform's verification system — opening up the once-rationed blue checks to anyone with eight dollars to spend very unwisely — was quickly turned into an exquisite carnival of shitposting with a *purpose*. People with the once-coveted checks changed their usernames and PFPs to impersonate the rich and famous, as well as the world's largest companies. Fake George W. Bush with a gamer tag tweeting:

I miss killing Iraqis ☹

while a fake Tony Blair quote-tweets that with a simple:

Same tbh.

A fake BP account saying:

Just cause we killed the planet doesn't mean we can't miss it ☹

Fake Nintendo of America tweeting an image of Mario giving the middle finger to the audience; one person sadly replied:

mario would never do that ☹

In return, the pantomime NoA said:

well he did

And, reader, he most assuredly did. Fake Roblox?

> were ading sex to roblox

Fake Coca-Cola?

> If this gets 1000 retweets we will put the cocaine back in Coca-Cola

Fake Nestlé?

> We steal your water and sell it back to you lol

There was also a richly deserved dunk on Tesla, whose fake account tweeted:

> Our cars do not respect school zone speed limits. Fuck them kids.

Finally, (since I read this tweet at the time, now you must as well) fake Rudy Giuliani tweeting:

> Nancy Pelosi and I do not agree on many things, but them things thangin I'll tell you what

The satirical possibilities enabled by buying an eight-dollar checkmark and impersonating everyone from corporations to ex-presidents were significant, making the case that Musk's plan was a disaster better than any lengthy explanation from self-serious commentators like me ever could. The impersonations helped ensure plenty of powerful people got mad at Musk at the same time, gave the press a bevy of examples of how misguided the proposal was, and even got some shots in at avaricious corporations like Eli Lilly, causing their stock price to tumble when an impersonator said insulin would be free:

> **Eli Lilly and Company** ☑
> **@EliLillyandCo**
> We are excited to announce insulin is free now
> **1:36 PM   11/1022 Twitter for iPhone**
> **554 Retweets 171 Quote Tweets 3,324 Likes**

A similar fate awaited Lockheed Martin:

> **Lockheed Martin** ☑
> **@LockheedMartini**
> We will begin halting all weapons sales to Saudi Arabia, Israel, and the United States until further investigation into their record of human rights abuses. #WeAreLM
>
>
>
> **8:19 PM 11/10/22 Twitter for Iphone**
> **175 Retweets 125 Quote Tweets 622 Likes**

What made this a rare example of successful Twitter activism was that it was training its sights on what was fundamentally a *problem with Twitter*, weaponizing the platform's affordances against the platform itself. To demonstrate how Musk's changes were idiotic, simply show the world how a bad actor would use them. This was something Twitter's veteran power users were intimately well-equipped to do. Cheaply and easily, with no dignity whatsoever, they told the truth about war criminals and corporations; it was a day-long cavalcade of ridiculously funny posts that were not only cathartic but meaningful. They put a dent in the stock market for a few minutes, generated a ton of bad press about Twitter, won the argument about this change to the platform, and above all utterly humiliated a man who paid $44 billion for this to happen to him. What it didn't change was the fact Musk owns the platform and remains in total control even after handing the company off to a gleefully self-humiliating puppet of a CEO.

***

This impersonation extravaganza was a fantastic way to go *out* — and as an old-school blue check myself, I honestly kind of regret not using the badge to impersonate some loathsome politician and get myself banned for the most glorious reasons imaginable. Some users explicitly said as much: if you're going to leave anyway, stick one in Musk's eye on the way out the door. But in time, this impersonation carnival began to be used to justify *staying*, because repeat episodes would hasten the site's demise.

One can see why this idea is tempting. After all, as of this writing at the tail end of 2023, Twitter's reported self-valuation is down to US$19 billion; Fidelity, which helped finance the takeover, puts the number as low as US$15 billion. But that's been driven by Musk's own chaotic anti-leadership of the company and his ceaseless descent into the most consequential case of Poster's Madness the world has ever seen.

This idea that shitposters (those who post in a deliberately ironic and provocative way) can tank a website's value by sticking around to frighten suburban mums, advertisers, and investors is another of those "just let me have this" illusions. Those who promulgate it often point to the period of Yahoo's ownership of Tumblr, when its users comforted themselves with the idea that it was all their shitposting, radical arguments, furry fan fiction, and erotic art that caused the site's value to drop dramatically by the time Yahoo cut its losses and sold the site on.

In fact, however, the reason Yahoo lost money on Tumblr was simply that they had dramatically overvalued it to begin with. Furry porn didn't tank Tumblr's value; it created it. People go where the furry porn is, and the presence of people is what makes a social media site look valuable. However, the very content that attracts them also makes the platform hard to sell as a mainstream property.

They were simply coming up against the perennial dilemma that a site's desirability to users is frequently inversely proportional to its marketability to advertisers. But when they tried to solve this by driving away the furry porn, they had nothing left.

In Musk's case, his Twitter eventually came back around to a more convoluted version of the previous verification policy, with unnecessary colour schemes, tiered price points ($1,000 for a *gold* checkmark!), and complex schemes for firms to sponsor their own employees for some kind of verification badge, complete with logos. This characterized a lot of Musk's other changes: pointless, Rube-Goldbergian in scope, and yet difficult to weaponize because of their inaccessibility.

Buying a checkmark to humiliate Musk via an Eli Lilly impersonation is pretty great, but if you buy one just to ensure your post drifts to the top the next time you want to own Ross Douthat in his replies, then at some point you're just paying Musk to do whatever he wants you to do on the platform. The tactics that worked so well as a surge of humiliation are now going to be channelled, however inefficiently, into producing value for the site. In a very real way, then, it's the same as it ever was.

When I think of the idea that we should shitpost harder here, I'm reminded of an old dril tweet:

go ahead. keep screaming "Shut The Fuck Up" at me. it only makes my opinions Worse.

Like the dril persona, Musk is immune, ultimately, to this kind of pressure. The decisions that are making Twitter worse, that make advertisers nervous, that generate bad publicity or outright break the site, are his and his alone. The idea that Twitter's implosion needs *you* to urge it along is a mirage.

***

At this point, Twitter is long past the point of redemption, and there is nothing to be gained by opposing Musk through the platform he owns. Many of us have, by now, heard some version of the following aggravating argument made by the most annoying and unoriginal people on the internet: "lol ur calling for the death of capitalism on ur iphone; but CAPITALISTS MADE THE iPHONE!" Changing society means participating in it. There is no escaping that. But sometimes the irony of participation really can overwhelm its possible virtues.

The reason why the "capitalists made the iPhone" fallacy is annoying is that it mistakes coercion for choice. We use the tools available to us to socialize and organize and simply survive. Getting by without a smartphone of some description these days is nearly impossible. The technology is a ubiquitous part of our lives; even in poor communities and developing nations, they've become indispensable tools for accessing the internet. The most unstinting of socialist organization is therefore going to pass through a smartphone at some point. You might as well upbraid a revolutionary for depending on clean water or a sewer system.

But not every tool is indispensable, and Twitter is not the iPhone. To be sure, there are a handful of people — mostly small-business-owners and freelancers — who rely on the enhancements provided by Twitter's network of influential people. One retweet, at the right time, from a famous author or actor or streamer can make you an absurd amount of money. But for most people on the platform, it is not truly *essential* — certainly not in the way that internet access per se is basically a utility at this point. Thus, there's no particular cruelty in pointing out that remaining on the platform is merely helping Elon Musk and achieving little else of value.

Abandoning the site to the terminally-unfunny, perennially-controversial far-right CHUDs that Musk has courted throughout this process will effectively render Twitter radioactive to the advertisers and VC money that he depends on. This process doesn't need you to help it out by staying on the site to undermine it. Indeed, if you're funny, sexy, charismatic, clever, or otherwise interesting, you may be helping to staunch the bleeding a bit. You're a star attraction, and sticking around may entice others to do the same rather than race to the nearest exit.

Are *you* the kind of person who creates real value for the platform? If so, it might be time to consider investing it elsewhere. By staying, you're providing reputational laundering for a sick platform that is corroding further by the hour. Your presence gives *other* people a reason to be there, and it gives news outlets an excuse to report on the goings-on at the site, as well as a reason for reporters, academics, and artists to hang out there as well. All of which makes Twitter influential, all of which magnifies the harms of its growing extremism-incubator, all of which increases its vexing value proposition.

Sure, there's no ethical consumption under capitalism, but that phrase isn't an ethical blank cheque either. Musk's ad revenue sharing scheme has sent cash transfers to mostly far-right Twitter Blue influencers. The creatively named "End Wokeness" account got US$10,400 from their first dump; Andrew Tate, currently under investigation by Romanian authorities for rape and sex trafficking, pocketed over US$20,000. It's worth asking if you want to be part of Andrew Tate's or Ian Miles Cheong's slush fund.

When we say there's no ethical consumption under capitalism, we mean that as a criticism of capitalism itself. Acquiring the tools to build a better world means buying some of them from a big-box retailer. But it doesn't mean you have to lend your shitposts, clout, and sexy-selfies to the business endeavours of every bigoted billionaire who turns up and buys some addictive platform. The last lever of power you truly have left as an individual that may hold a glimmer of hope for doing *some* good here is to simply walk away.

***

So much for post-Musk Twitter. But there remains a more challenging argument to make. What if, through some quantum swerve, a court case going a different way perhaps, Musk had pulled out and never bought Twitter? What if he hadn't hacked the site to pieces? What if Twitter was still like it used to be? Even then, I'd argue, you should still log off.

Twitter became valuable because it was where "the world has a conversation" — or a "global consciousness," in a typically woo Jack Dorsey phrase. Except it wasn't *the world*. It was an unrepresentative slice thereof.* It's not just that the site's power users were unrepresentative of their local populations in demographic terms; it's also that the power users were disproportionately what I call the *epistemic elite* — famous artists, writers, journalists, critics, and academics; powerful political operatives; local civil servants; the Pope; prime ministers; celebrities, every non-profit you'd care to name, local transit agencies, c-suite

....

* According to the Pew Research Center, in 2023, approximately 23 percent of Americans say they "ever" use Twitter, and out of that 23 percent, only 20 percent of US adults on the site produce an astonishing 98 percent of American tweets. This works out to fewer than 5 percent of Americans being high-volume posters you're likely to see on the platform. According to a 2019 analysis from Pew, Twitter users are "younger, more likely to identify as Democrats, more highly educated and have higher incomes than U.S. adults overall." While that's likely changed since late 2022, the shift would almost certainly skew things towards a similarly unrepresentative slice of Republicans.

executives and the corporations they ran. This was what made the site the centre of so many conversations — and what made it so dangerous as a vector of disinformation.

Twitter didn't matter so much without these people (and all those who followed them on the platform). But all of these powerful individuals, constantly doomscrolling with the rest of us, absorbing the ugliness, the mis/disinformation, the drumbeat of fringe views from every quarter, also experienced the same distortion of reality as the rest of us: we assigned outsize importance to views, people, or phenomena we wouldn't have given the time of day to had we not been compulsively scrolling.

Unlike most garden-variety users, however, these epistemic elites have the unique capacity to make Twitter's bullshit *everyone's* bullshit in a matter of hours. While Twitter's plague of disinformation will negatively affect everyone who logs on, it's the veteran journalists who force it in front of everyone else's eyeballs on the front pages and in the prime-time television spots, ensuring the Not Extremely Online majority *also* has to hear about the latest Twitter beef or the newest conspiracy theory. As is so often the case, the press's fixation on online drama is a reflection of a peculiar species of narcissism that turns their own dramas into matters of National Importance. What happens to *people like them* in the wilds of social media belongs on the front page. Not so much the rest of us.

Does anyone truly believe that the mainstream press would've become obsessed with the nonsense un-debate about "pregnant people" as a trans-sensitive term if a disproportionate number of coastal journalists weren't watching Leon_Thotsky and RipVanTwinkle420 argue about such issues and other extremely esoteric points of lefty dis-agreement? Where would Pamela Paul's *New York Times* column be without Twitter users in their twenties and thirties having extremely abstract debates about such esoterica, making it all seem far more pervasive than it really is? Who would she blame for the downfall of Western civilization? She might have to actually look out her window for a change.*

The entire trans language debate struck me as a farce, because no one except people on Twitter and in the editorial pages of the *New York Times* were talking about it.[6] When people like *Times* journalists started following, say, the Twitter rantings of J.K. Rowling, who whinged endlessly about the issue (remember her "Wumben" tweet? I wish I didn't!)[7] the consequences were dire. It could only tragically distort their perspectives in ways that led them to paint a target on trans people's backs, assigning this debate a level of importance, pervasiveness, and influence that was not reflected anywhere in reality.

....

* As of this writing, New York, my hometown, is blanketed under a choking haze of wildfire smoke from Québec, so here's hoping that if Paul did look out her window, she finally alighted on a real problem to write about — and that she doesn't blame trans women for the haze.

But since Leon_Thotsky and JK Rowling: Twitter Edition loomed large in the consciousness of a lot of writers, editors, and journalists, it all looked much more significant than it really was. It's hardly a coincidence that the most overtly transphobic stenographers (men like Jesse Singal, for instance) or their transphobia-curious enablers (like Matt Yglesias or Jonathan Chait) are Extremely Online, with expansive Twitter presences and followings the size of small cities.

On a platform where trans people are ourselves disproportionately represented — and where, therefore, our *arguments* about endless trivia are disproportionately represented — it gives people like this, who are primed to be obsessed with us and our discourse, an easy way to access it and then misrepresent it in their work. This, itself, is a symptom of something I've also occasionally been guilty of — harvesting tweets as a substitute for journalism. It's just easier and cheaper to source evidence from a site you're already addicted to, and using as some perverse and corrosive substitute for fun, than to carry out any sort of actual investigative journalism.

But it's also part of a larger problem where many lefty Twitter users use the platform *as if* it's not the open platform that it is, where literally anyone can see what you're saying as long as they have the link. This is a problem for everyone, of course; we *all* use open platforms as if we're whispering to our best friend. Or as if we're shouting into the void, if you prefer. But we're also aggregating our intimate, awkward, imperfect conversations in a place where obsessive bad actors can find them.

Consider the way the toxicity of "YA Twitter" (the name given to the cluster of Twitter users who write and/or read young adult novels) became a *thing* in a variety of outlets — from *New York* magazine to the *New Yorker*, to *Reason*, to *Vulture*, to the *New York Times*, to *Tablet*. Or perhaps consider the *New York Times Magazine* "Bad Art Friend" piece that brought to nationwide attention interpersonal drama that began in chatrooms and spilled onto social media. Both of these examples involve authors who might be said, in some sense, to have it coming to them. But the press's Eye of Sauron is not so discriminating: it also alights on purely innocent, ordinary people who have never written a book in their life. The consequences can be dire.

For instance, "Plane Bae," the unfortunate 2018 episode that involved an unsuspecting, telegenic man and woman on a cross-country flight who were spied on by an aspiring comedienne who then creatively live-tweeted how she was shipping these two strangers who'd struck up the kind of awkward conversation that bedevils too many of us on long-haul flights. Numerous bits of running commentary from the comedienne followed, like:

No wedding rings in sight!!!!!!

or the absolutely vital:

> Breaking. They just left for the bathroom at
> the SAME TIME.

And, of course, just outright eavesdropping:

> Guess what they have both been talking
> nonstop since we took off. They're both
> personal trainers. They have touched arms a
> number of times. They are both vegetarians.

The result was not merely a viral Twitter storm that would embarrass even the sluttiest, most gregarious soul, but an ensuing take-up by mainstream news sources the world over, leading in turn to interviews and lavish special interest stories in venues such as ABC's *Good Morning America*, among others. Which, of course, in turn resulted in the poor young woman in question being harassed viciously when she refused to play her part in the fan-fiction Twitter had written about her. She was not, it turns out, romantically interested in her seatmate. And all this happened because far too many people such as TV producers and on-air personalities were spending too much time on Twitter and *saw this nonsense in the first place.*

Such people — media people with ready access to the press and more traditional platforms — should be well positioned to explain how harmful this dynamic is, yet few do — perhaps because we'd implicate ourselves or seem hypocritical given the benefits to our careers. Well, let me state here and now that I was a hypocrite. I personally benefitted from my Twitter use, as did my career. I have at least two and arguably three girlfriends as a result of the platform, to say nothing of uncounted interview opportunities, writing gigs, speaking gigs, and so much more besides.

But then, that's all Twitter was ever good for. A ceaseless state lottery in which the only way to win was to play, to reap *individual* benefits. A little more money, a little more attention, a few more conversations with the right people. I can't deny that I benefitted from that, but I also won't justify it as anything more than it was. Something *I* needed for myself, my nesting partner, and my cats. It wasn't worthwhile for *society*. I mean, I *hope* my extended Twitter lectures might've convinced a few people of some noble or worthwhile idea. But even if they did, it's a small benefit gained for far too dear a price — both to my mental health and to society at large.

* * *

Twitter was bad in its bones long before Musk's takeover. If it remains a widely used app, however, Musk's ceaseless, embarrassing courtship of the far right will only make it worse. If we're to think of things from an appropriately labour-focused perspective, then we might recognize ourselves as the generators of any given platform's profit. The film-negative of "you are the product" is "you are the value." Your little bons mots, your memes, your gems of conversation, your shitposting, your non-specific wit, all make a given platform valuable. You help create the Jovian mass that attracts others to a site. They want to see *your* bullshit; or, perhaps more aptly, your *participation* in a collective of bullshit. How many times have we looked at a hilarious Twitter thread specifically to see everyone *else's* witty reactions to something?

That's what you're bringing, and it's what keeps Twitter relevant and newsworthy. You need to deny it the value of your posting, the gift and newsworthiness of your presence. As *New Yorker* writer Jelani Cobb put it, "to the extent that people remain active on Twitter, they preserve the fragile viability of Musk's gambit. The illusory sense of community that still lingers on the platform is one of Musk's most significant assets."[8]

Only when you do your part to dissolve that illusory community will Twitter finally achieve its inevitable destiny of becoming 4chan: The Blog. It'll still be dangerous, in the way that 4chan itself, and its lesser spawn of 8chan/8kun, has been; or perhaps Twitter will become something akin to Stormfront. But, in every case, monitoring can be left to extremism experts at places like the Southern Poverty Law Center, and the platform can cease to function as the fig-leaf justification that addicts use to remain glued to the site's doomscroll. *You* do not owe the petty, evil people on this platform the gift of your undivided attention.

The Revolution Will Not Be Shitposted

Following Elon Musk's Twitter takeover, a curious genre of platform obituary arose in the mainstream media. The nerdiest versions bewailed the loss of a valuable source of information. "Twitter was for news," lamented Alex Kirshner at *Slate*.[9] The *Guardian*'s Johana Bhuiyan eulogized, "For us emerging reporters, it was the place where you could post your unhinged thoughts right after sharing your latest investigative story. It was the place you went to find real-time updates on major news events and takes on the latest media drama."[10]

Slightly cooler journalists, however, usually emphasized something else: Twitter's humour. The *Guardian*'s Lois Beckett reflected on a 2018 report of hers that saw her hole up for a week with no social media access, recounting that "the stunt backfired: living alone for days in a picturesque cabin, reading a dozen well-researched volumes, only reminded me of how dazzling and entertaining and unexpected Twitter could be."[11]

Allison Johnson, over at the *Verge*, was perhaps even more lachrymose:

> Twitter gave us all so much. It helped us keep tabs on Pépito the cat. It allowed us to laugh at and circulate the dumbest jokes imaginable. It united us all in the sheer ecstasy of two llamas evading capture. Sure, there were trolls... But it turned into something kind of great. A place where funny weirdos and smart people hung out.[12]

They don't use the word, but the thing they're talking about is shitposting. And they're not exactly wrong. Twitter was a hub of shitposting, much as sites like 4chan or Something Awful or Newgrounds* had been in the generation before. However, those sites had been intimidatingly unwelcoming black boxes full of young, masked, and mysterious edgelords. Twitter, by contrast, was hyper-accessible and directly plugged into establishment media. Twitter took shitposting mainstream.

On a basic level, shitposts (in the unlikely event you're unfamiliar with the term) are where

....

* Newgrounds is a little hard to describe, but imagine an early You-Tube where you could also play video games. Everything ran on Flash, and it was a place to see (and comment and vote on) all manner of original videos, music videos, and tons and tons of original anima-tion—much of which was uncensored. From anti-Iraq War content to animations based on memes from the Something Awful or 4chan forums to homemade adventure games, it all lived here. It still exists, too! But as with most such sites, there was nothing like being there when it was a veritable Times Square of assaultive new culture.

people who are good at the internet show off their skill by doing parodic renditions of people who are bad at the internet. They're a kind of digital *sprezzatura*: a studied dishevelment of language that takes great effort to produce, despite looking completely careless — deliberately misspelled, free from the constraints of punctuation, and, above all, irreverent. A shitpost might be a really specific bitchy rant about someone's co-workers, except halfway through you realize they're talking about the characters in *Scooby-Doo*. It might be an inspirational "live, love, laugh"-style meme, except in favour of eating sand and giving yourself a bezoar. It's the genre that gave us all the 9/11 jokes that are actually funny and the trend of PhD students calling themselves bimbos. It's an endless series of experimental beakers overflowing with gags (and bimboification gas). The one rule, if you can call it that, is to not appear to take *anything* seriously. Sincerity is anathema to shitposting.

As such, the desire of the media Twitter eulogists to somehow ennoble shitposting is as deeply against the spirit of the shitposter as it is possible to be. When former NBC tech journalist Ben Collins, for instance, argues (on Twitter, appropriately enough) that "[shitposters are] an enforcement mechanism that allows for better conversations and shoos away hate," he could not be missing the point more.

Yes, mockery can be situationally powerful. As media critic Lindsay Ellis once observed, there's a reason Nazis frequently emulate the aesthetics of productions like *American History X* — which flatters them as dangerous badasses even as it purports to seriously criticize them — but *never* imitate *The Producers*, which reveals the "shoddy theatricality" of fascism.[13] Shitposters can be like a non-stop performance of *The Producers* when it comes to mocking truly horrid people. But they also can be, and often are, toxic and abusive, harassing other users for kicks because they had the audacity to care about something *without* disguising it behind layers of *bien pensant* irony. There is no requirement that shitposters shitpost for worthy causes. Indeed, their avocation often requires the very opposite.

The hope that, even if we can't salvage the Twitter that broke world news (in both senses of the term), we might nevertheless salvage, of all things, *shitposting* and unleash its supposed political power represents one of the more desperate grabs onto the floating-*Titanic*-door of Web 2.0. It's a hope that is misguided not only about Twitter but also about, even more crucially, the actual purpose of shitposting.

***

There are many possible avatars of shitposting, but Twitter's dril, whose laconically weird posts have become a kind of Marcus Aurelius's *Meditations* for Web 2.0, is always a useful place to start. Especially now that we are in a position to chart both his rise *and* his fall.

Long before the Musk episode, dril was already a minor civic deity for Twitter — the equivalent of what Athena means to Athens, or Gritty to Philadelphia. Some bangers include:

> "jail isnt real," i assure myself as i close my eyes and ram the hallmark gift shop with my shitty bronco

> another day volunteering at the betsy ross museum. everyone keeps asking me if they can fuck the flag. buddy, they wont even let me fuck it

> ah, So u persecute Jared Fogle just because he has different beliefs? Do Tell. (girls get mad at me) Sorry. Im sorry. Im trying to remove it

> IF THE ZOO BANS ME FOR HOLLERING AT THE ANIMALS I WILL FACE GOD AND WALK BACKWARDS INTO HELL

And, of course, my personal favourite:

> "This Whole Thing Smacks Of Gender," i holler as i overturn my uncle's barbeque grill and turn the 4th of July into the 4th of Shit

This is shitposting's Weberian ideal-type, right down to the misspellings, psychedelic syntax, and chaotic grammar.

When Musk purchased Twitter, this civic deity came to his community's defence, most notably by throwing his weight behind a hashtag meant to encourage widespread blocking of all users credulous enough to pay for Musk's $8-a-month "Twitter Blue" service:

```
you just paid $8 to eat my ass stupid
#BlockTheBlue
```

After that, Musk appeared to foist a blue checkmark on dril without his consent. Through repeated ironic name changes, in violation of terms of service designed to put a halt to the wave of impersonations discussed above, dril was able to get rid of it, but not before mocking Musk at great length:

slave to Woke @dril · 10h ☑
now that i have the baneful blue mark, I understand the pain ive wrought. i was wrong to torment dog coin guys. im jealous of their million's
336 replies 6078 retweets
72.1K likes 3.2M impressions

slave to Woke @dril · 10h ☑
building a pressurized 3000 mile long tube across the desert instead of a normal train is actually a really good idea. Always has been
81 replies 5,216 retweets
55K likes 1.3M impressions

slave to Woke @dril · 10h ☑
you can disaggrree with Jeffrey Epstein
and Ghislane Maxwells politics while still
hanging out with them in photographs Its
totally fine
532 replies 10.3K retweets
68.1K likes 2.1M impressions

It was, indeed, glorious to watch the consummate poster turn his satirical skills on Musk, a man who could never be a fraction of the poster he so dearly wished to be. At the same time, though, dril was committing a cardinal sin against shitposting culture: he was showing the world that he cared about something.

The karmic retribution was swift and merciless. Dril helped get #BlockTheBlue trending, but this quickly led to backlash from some sex workers (and, more to the point, many others who claimed to speak for them) who argued that because visibility was crucial to sex workers' livelihoods, many had purchased Twitter Blue to ensure they weren't downranked.

This was true up to a point. As is so often the case with this style of hectoring activism, one should be wary of those claiming to speak for a whole community of such diverse people. Many sex workers did not purchase Twitter Blue. More importantly, there's no evidence #BlockTheBlue had any significant impact on those sex workers who did — or, for that matter, on anyone at all. The campaign failed even to identify a meaningful common practice. Did you just block one by one? On a case-by-case basis with a bias towards blocking? Did you use a blocklist or some other tool? Who could say? Like most gestural activism of its ilk, its primary purpose was to signal affiliation (and stir up a little harassment, as some innocent people were yelled at by sanctimonious blue-blockers) not to have an effect

This backlash wasn't even confined to Twitter. It formed such a perfectly closed loop of shelf-stable online Discourse that when, months later, dril started a Bluesky account, waves of chatter about his supposedly vicious anti-sex work activism followed him. The entire saga as it manifested on Bluesky was grim to watch: a vicious argument with precious little substance.

By saying things he *meant* on Twitter, dril opened himself to callouts that have permanently branded him anti-sex worker for something that had no material impact on sex workers whatever. All in the name of a gestural "action" in which it could be said that he was, at worst, ignorant of the fact that *some* sex workers had tried to use Twitter Blue to maintain their networks. No sex workers were helped, a lot of people pointlessly yelled at one another about any and everything, with escalating allegations held up by loftier abstractions, and then, as is so often the case, it faded away. In any event, no one learned anything.

But what this really demonstrates is the limits of shitposting. That dril elected *not* to ignore Musk's destruction of Twitter is perhaps the least shitposty thing he's ever done — and much to his credit. But by showing sincerity, by engaging in something like *activism*, dril finally made himself "cancellable" in the eyes of the kind of Twitter user — the polar opposite, one might say, of the shitposter — whose social media tactics revolve around weaponized sincerity.

Worst of all, dril stopped being funny, as if some magic seal had been broken by his disastrous foray into activism. When he appeared on Bluesky, I almost didn't believe it was him; his posts were so defensive, bitter, and unfunny. There was none of that digital *sprezzatura*. They were entirely *too* studied. For instance,

```
just spoke with the mods... they said theyre
adding DMs on this web site as soon as they
get one user who people actually want to
talk to
```

This is what dril became.

As he stepped back from gestural activism, his posts began to improve once again — perhaps dril cannot be killed, even by himself — but the episode, in its bitterness and futility, shows that even the best posters will be buried by the inadequacies of online activism.

When you're funny online, you can feel incredibly powerful, able to move mountains and deflect the attacks of even the most self-important, priggish busybodies. But politics demands a soupçon of seriousness, and once you start going down that road, futility soon follows. After all, the only thing you can do with the sincerity required to *be* an activist online is weaponize it.

***

It's worth taking a second to define *weaponized sincerity*. Weaponized sincerity is where extreme takes are born. It's a mode that deploys ever more esoteric manipulations of social justice concepts for the purpose of being edgy or controversial, while still earnestly pursuing some noble idea. It's the o-to-6o-in-two-seconds-flat acceleration of an innocuous bit of posting into a mass callout. It's being nebulously accused of being X-phobic or silencing Y-group or being imperialist when all you were doing was, for instance, delivering chili to your neighbours.

One evening in 2022, a relatively prominent lefty Twitter user posted the following:

> several guys moved in next door, students I guess. and I've gotten two confused doordash drivers for them in the last week, and their trash can was completely overflowing with pizza boxes. i don't think they cook. i am feeling such a strange motherly urge to feed these boys... They're incredibly quiet which is a real surprise. I dunno if they're renting or what but I would like them to stick around. Maybe I will make a big pot of chili this weekend when it gets cooler.

This, somehow, ignited a firestorm. She was accused of coddling "manchildren," of being "presumptuous" or otherwise rude, of ableism for ignoring potential allergies, and of being a white saviour.

> For the love of god, stop babying men. This is why they learn to take advantage of their wives

went one tweet, apparently blaming this woman for the endurance of sexism and unequal marriages. Another tweet read, in part,

> The intent was good, right? No. It was presumptive and stereotypical [white people] shit.

The harassment went on for days.

It was a flaming gout of internet rage that reached into the stratosphere of the mainstream press. Even the *Washington Post* reported on the controversy — and it got its money's worth from the world's most efficient content farm. The article wasn't just a news report; it was an *advice column*. *WaPo* food reporter Emily Heil used the incident to ask etiquette experts for their opinions on how best to share food with strangers.

> The social media food fight left us exhausted but also wondering: Have the rules for giving home-cooked foods changed? Does the

simple act of baking a casserole or cookies for a stranger have to be so fraught? We asked two experts for guidance.

Imagine the horror of having such an innocuous post lead to three people you've never met dissecting your behaviour in the pages of a national newspaper.

In the event, the leftist in question delivered the chili, it was well-received, and the young men helped her fix a fence. Outside the swirling cyclone of Discourse, a rather ordinary and charming exchange took place. On Twitter, this pot of chili had to be saddled with the unbearable weight of some of the most important issues of our time. Even a Le Creuset can't hold *that*.

But, worst of all, because most of the *Washington Post*'s newsroom is on Twitter, they made this sorry spectacle into everyone's problem. Even New York City's Fox affiliate got in on the action, with an article entitled "A Chili Controversy? Neighbor's Good Deed Draws Online Outrage." Their source was the *Washington Post*.

***

I'm talking as if weaponized sincerity was the opposite of shitposting, its natural enemy. And in one sense it is. But, like all true opposites, it's also a twin. Weaponized sincerity is the horrible second helix that wraps around irony culture, feeding off it and nourishing it in equal measure.

It's all deadly serious, of course. Unlike the shitposter's jokey, over-the-top irony, the tool of weaponized sincerity is grave, over-the-top earnestness. It leverages the potential of taking platforms *way* too seriously; irony poisoning arises from strenuously pretending that you're *not* doing that. And so, of course, mocking earnest-posters is a major hobby of shitposters:

brandon access memories
@uncledoomer
go ahead. post another "take." tell me that eating hot dogs is ableist. say jackbox games doesn't center bipoc voices. accuse a famous person of grooming their younger spouse. come up with a woke way to say race mixing is wrong. call me gay for liking dessert.

7:24 am   August 10, 2020   Twitter for iPhone

Over on Bluesky, as of this writing, one can find shitposters laughing at, for instance, people who — in all apparent sincerity — argued that hating

NFTs was bigotry because, allegedly, some queer people used them to evade homelessness. Another user, a hand-wringing white woman, asked a Black shitposter if it was okay for her to like one of her jokey tweets because it had the n-word in it. And still another, a white non-binary person, sonorously lectured The Vagina Museum's Bluesky account that they ought not to violate the "posting strike" that was being observed (by virtually no one who mattered) in protest of Bluesky's lax moderation policies. The Museum promptly left Bluesky in protest, while remaining on Twitter and Facebook (those infamously non-racist sites that have not contributed to prejudice in any way whatsoever).

It's all very Late Twitter, evincing a particular kind of posting disease. But, for our purposes, it's enough to note that all of this was mocked with winks and nods and ass-posting by the shitposters. The shitposter can posture as genre-savvy, too cool to make those sorts of cringey takes. Except, of course, when they could justify it to themselves. The same people who mocked that nervous white lady for her walking on eggshells and the way it othered Black posters often took no responsibility for throwing the eggshells on the ground in the first place — thereby creating an environment where people of one privileged background or another, desperate to "play by the rules" and "do the right thing," were inevitably going to behave in ways that would fetishize or other people of colour, queer people, trans people, and so on.

There is, in truth, no bright line between shitposters and those who weaponize sincerity. They're often the same crowd, moving between the two roles when it's convenient, and loudly protesting either their savviness or their sincerity when it suits them. At every stage they'll use their own erstwhile comrades as foils for whatever they happen to be touting at that particular moment. It's another closed system.

I might even go a little further. These kinds of aggressively earnest takes lend themselves so well to adoption as shitposting memes because, in their courting of edginess, their engagement in a kind of arms race of rhetorical excess, their own perverse pursuit of some twisted kind of digital dishevelment, they are so close to it already.

To return to our prior chili example. The leftist woman in question raised pigs for fun — so someone thought it would be funny to threaten to kill and cook her pigs. Is this weaponized sincerity or is it shitposting? The internet has made it risible to quote Orwell, but in this case one can't help but think, "The creatures outside looked from pig to man, and from man to pig, and from pig to man again; but already it was impossible to say which was which."

***

I remain fascinated by how it is that people who present themselves as being too cool to post silly, Extremely Online takes inevitably end up doing precisely that when it suits them. It's a particular twist on a theory I've used to explain online harassment: the Möbius strip of reality and unreality. A Möbius strip is a one-sided mathematical object that gives the illusion of having two sides, looking a bit like an infinity symbol. You can draw a line on the Möbius strip's entire side without ever lifting the pen from the surface.

To wit, the way people justify bad behaviour online often boils down to a simple proposition: the internet is real when I need it to be, and it's "just" the internet when I don't.

This is a pattern that came up again and again in my studies of online harassment. A gamer would rage at his teammates in an online game, blaming them when they lost a match — peppering his tirade with ethnic and sexual slurs — and then would argue that none of what he said mattered, none of it was "real" abuse, because it was "just a game." It was mere trash talk. The internet was real enough to justify this gamer's outrage at losing a match, but unreal when he needed to pretend his words and deeds in response were consequence-free.

Similarly, if I'm a jerk to someone on social media and they express hurt or outrage, I can simply say, "Suck it up, buttercup, it's just the internet." If someone is a jerk to *me* and makes me cry, I can scream bloody murder about how words online are devastating to my feelings and my mental health. Real when it's convenient, unreal when it's not. A Möbius strip.

Anyone who's ever been Extremely Online has indulged in this shell game to one degree or another, justifying our edgy fun to ourselves regardless of who gets hurt, while also wailing in distress whenever we come across something *we ourselves* dislike. More specifically, and as I've argued, shitposters and cringey earnest-posters are very often the same people: ironic when that's advantageous, too serious by half when it isn't. But where these two forces come together at their very worst is when the Discourse in question is about a specific *person*.

***

Occasionally this can be valorous, mocking a fascist or some waste of skin who called the cops on a Black person who looked at her funny. In those moments, the shitposter-turned-serious who uses their art to dunk on someone can take on the cast of Robin Hood, stealing dignity from the bastards and redistributing bits of it to all the rest of us. At their best, a good shitposter can deflate the pretensions of some extremist or a would-be desk-murderer who takes themselves too seriously.

But even then, shitposting has its limitations. Take the case of reactionary centrist pundit Matt Yglesias, who, as of this writing, has done more than his fair share to propagate transphobic narratives circulating in the media — for instance, helping to fuel the wildly overcooked controversy about a gender clinic for minors in St. Louis, which led to the clinic being closed and fuelled the march of transphobic legislation in Missouri. In one Substack post (where else?) he argued that the right-wing spectre of a massive surge in young cis girls being cajoled into developing trans identities might really have something to it. "We are now," he writes, "in a new era of medicalizing teen girls' discomfort with patriarchy while downplaying what appears to be a widespread youth mental health crisis." He has also claimed that a "very rapid increase in the number of children identifying as trans raises questions about the extent to which the use of gender-affirming medications has been clinically studied."[14] I could go on, but it's the usual "reasonable" concern-trolling about this issue. The number of minors in the US who receive any kind of gender-affirming care remains vanishingly small.

Obviously, this has rather annoyed a lot of us internet trannies. But much as I sympathize with the young trans woman who welcomed Yglesias to Bluesky by skeeting

WE ARE GOING TO BEAT YOU WITH HAMMERS

at him, thus getting herself banned, it's hard for me to see what was accomplished by her action. Social media makes it trivially easy to prize momentary catharsis and, worse, to *ennoble* it. That catharsis — to which we as marginalized people have an unassailable moral right (because what the hell else do we get?) — can easily become a licence for all manner of abusive behaviour. Up to and including violent threats.

A pie in Anita Bryant's face at least had the virtue of happening in person, on camera. Same with glitterbombing. It was daring. It took courage. And the semiotics were *choice*. It was humiliating, but also fundamentally unthreatening: a pie in the face is a classic comic symbol for a silly come-uppance; glitter is more or less the opposite of an actual bomb. The reason these sorts of public humiliations work is that they contrast the brutality of the target with the silliness of their would-be victims — a gesture that calls for peace, masquerading as violence, all of which deflates the pretensions of the inevitably self-serious target. For a bigot to say their life was threatened by custard just compounds the humiliation.

But an online threat to beat someone with a deadly weapon has an altogether different valence — and it makes *you* seem churlish when you claim martyrdom for being banned for an obvious terms-of-service violation.

Hammer-gate became just another same-shit-different-day episode on open social media that neatly accorded with the way people like Yglesias see the world. Despite his best efforts, he is not an idiot. He knows that a lot of people dislike him and his concern-trolling approach to a dozen and one issues of vital importance; and, in partic-ular, he's very aware that trans people resent his pedantic JAQ-ing off about trans health care. So, once again, I have to ask what the hammer skeet accomplished other than ensuring that one of the very first people Bluesky had to ban was a trans woman.

***

Moreover, even that questionable scenario is the exception that proves the rule. Far more often, when the average shitposter decides to prove to both themselves and their audience that they're truly on the side of the angels, and not merely some microblogging jester whose mockery of all things sincere also rides roughshod over genuinely emancipatory politics, they look to people closer to home as target dummies. Consequently, most people who take their turn in the Discourse Oubliette are neither famous nor able to handle the tide of strangers crashing against their lives with imprecations and allegations.

Thus, although the online trans community comes in for rather more than its fair share of harassment from outsiders, we're also perfectly adept at destroying each other without their help. Periodically, a group of us will find another person to tie to a digital Catherine-wheel in the hopes of proving — if only to ourselves — that our marrow-deep irony poisoning hasn't stopped us from identifying "bad guys" and meting out a condign punishment to them. This sort of thinking was what led to the ordeal of a trans woman spec-fic writer, Isabel Fall.

Fall was a first-time sci-fi writer and managed to get her debut story published in *Clarkesworld* — a huge accomplishment in this small world. She titled her military sci-fi story, a tale of mechs, identity, and imperialism, "I Sexually Identify as an Attack Helicopter," an obvious play on a frequently used transphobic anti-joke. Fall also had the unfortunate distinction of being born in 1988, and of that being one of the scant details she included in her all too brief bio.

The revulsion expressed by some people who read only the story's provocative title was extreme. Soon after, they latched on to the birth-date. As many know, "88" is an old neo-Nazi code for "HH," short for "Heil Hitler." A number of Twitter users across a broad spectrum of online communities — Book Twitter, Sci-Fi Twitter, Trans Twitter, and the various flavours of shit-posting subcultures that were endemic to all the above and more — became convinced that the story was a hoax planted by a Nazi who had pulled one over on Clarkesworld to publish a secretly anti-trans story in one of the English language's most important sci-fi journals.

This narrative developed the momentum of a miles-long freight train, sweeping up even big names in sci-fi who condemned the magazine. All the while, Fall was reading what her own community — including many, many authors she looked up to and had been inspired by — were saying about her and her work online. It was no surprise that she was pushed to the edge of suicide.

In January 2020 *Clarkesworld* editor Neil Clarke wrote a lengthy response to the farrago saying:

> Isabel's bio is intentionally short and internet presence negligible. I understand that to be a common practice for trans people who are wary of attacks from anti-trans campaigners. Unfortunately, the same shield used against them opened her up to an unexpected attack from others.

He went on to add,

> Furthermore, Isabel was not out as trans when this story was published. Various claims being made against her pressured Isabel into publicly outing herself as a defence against the attacks. That should never be the case and is very disturbing to me. Isabel was born in 1988. That does not make one a neo-Nazi. I'm honestly surprised and disappointed that I have to say that.

My own role in the Fall saga was minimal. I expressed private scepticism about the story at the time. I didn't post publicly about it, nor join the mob campaign against her, but I also didn't question it. I fell into the same trap as many others: What if it really *was* a hoax? I didn't want to look like a fool. Least of all someone fooled by *Nazis*. My pride, and my assurance in what I thought I knew of far-right tactics, stilled my voice.

Once Fall came out as trans, I felt I should've said something. That I should've defended her. That I should've known better. But the really fucked-up part is that if I had, it might not have helped at all. I'd have started some arguments and gotten some people angry at me. But I wouldn't have slowed the avalanche descending on Isabel Fall's life with grim inevitability. On the contrary, I would probably have contributed to it.

The kind of guilt I was feeling can itself, in the context of social media, become dangerous. After it came out that Fall was really trans and not a Nazi, a segment of people who had either been right about her all along, or who were feeling deeply penitent for having been wrong about her, decided the best next step was to harass a variety of people they (mis)identified as "ringleaders" of the anti-Fall harassment campaign.

Unsurprisingly, many of the targets here were prominent people of colour in the world of sci-fi, people who'd made the odd ill-advised (and regretted) tweet about Isabel Fall, but who could not be considered ringleaders by any stretch of the imagination. They were just people who'd been duped, like so many others, or people like me who didn't say what was right for fear of being wrong on the internet. And so, the wheel of social media harassment turned yet another time — another exercise in proving our moral rectitude by attacking and attempting to destroy yet another individual or three. Canned justice, now available in Costco-sized pallets.

***

As of today, Fall has stopped writing publicly and become reclusive.[15] For too many trans people, our first introduction to the online communities we so depend on (and online is all that, with our microscopic numbers, allows us to *become* a community) is an act of hazing. Introduction to one's own community should not be discussed in terms of *survivorship*, yet it's what the terrible logic of social media has rapidly accelerated.

I experienced it myself way back in 2009 when I started trans-blogging. It didn't take very long at all for me to put my foot in it, and this resulted in another trans woman telling me she hoped a dear friend of mine died from her terminal illness. Painfully. Welcome to the community! Except I stayed, and Isabel is gone.

As my story illustrates, this phenomenon didn't start with Twitter. My own harrowing occurred on LiveJournal. But one needs Twitter to destroy someone as thoroughly as we destroyed Isabel Fall, to network numerous famous and influential people, along with the international media, to the gaggle of shitposters and nobodies dogpiling a potentially newsworthy target. My unpleasant encounter involved, at most, half a dozen people in LiveJournal comments. Fall's involved hundreds — including authors she grew up reading. I don't know if I could've survived a harrowing of *that* intensity.

As journalist and critic Emily St. James put it so well in *Vox*, apropos of the Fall saga:

> what this story really symbolizes is the fact that as we've grown more adept at using the internet, we've also grown more adept at destroying people's lives, but from a distance, in an abstracted way.

There are no brakes, no speed bumps, nothing to stop a sufficiently viral campaign from spreading everywhere and smothering your reputation beneath it. *That* is what Twitter and TikTok can facilitate, and it is arguably *the* defining feature of Web 2.0.

***

So many of these stories, from the ballad of dril's decline to the harassment of Isabel Fall, are in some sense the same story. They follow the mad-lib logic of internet drama, a formula perfectly designed to sweep up the well-meaning who don't realize how Extremely Online they've become. Just tell them they're saving the world or, as Ben Collins would have it, that they're "shooing away hate" with their edginess.

In all cases, the basic issue is that too many people are mistaking posting (whether earnest- or shit-) for praxis. But Web 2.0 social media is not any sort of reasonable substitute for far more substantial forms of activism and labour. It's far easier to dunk on the day's Main Character* than to do the slow, boring work of community building and maintenance. The bitter irony for trans communities is that this squanders the very gift that social media gave us: the ability to build meaningful, international communities *at all*.

On the contrary, such community policing crusades usually end up targeting the most vulnerable. Despite their ostensible purpose — defence of the most marginalized — they achieve the opposite, redoubling discriminatory forces and turning marginalized people *against* one another. That truth hits you like a speeding bus if you spend enough time on these platforms. Consider this *cri de coeur* of a post from Bluesky:

> stg 90% of my role in discourses is "your anger is valid, but for the love of GOD aim the anger at the right fucking people for ONCE. the person in front of you is NOT the one that's fucking you. we are a group of leftists who call each other fascists more often than we call actual fascists fascists."

....

* The term derives from a 2019 tweet by Twitter user, ahem, maple cocaine, who wrote: "Each day on twitter there is one main character. The goal is to never be it." This referred to the way an individual user would often trend on certain days for negative reasons — like "Bean Dad," the father who refused to feed his child in order to compel her to learn how to use a can opener entirely on her own. Sometimes the Main Character is a cad or a racist. Sometimes they're just awkward. Sometimes they're an innocent person caught up in viral forces they can't control. In any event, becoming a Main Character is how you get known as Velveeta Cooking Wine Lady for the rest of your life (that's a made-up example; if it's not, please don't write to me about it).

They're talking about horizontal hostility, and the fact that our mighty weapons of "accountability" on these platforms tend to be trained on each other rather than on fascists. Part of the reason for that is that, quite simply, we're more readily available to one another; we care more, because it stings to be accused of violating our deeply held values. A far-right extremist or some garden-variety bigot is less apt to give a damn. We hurt each other with our words precisely because we *can* be hurt by them.

Much has been made recently, by those discussing the illusory rhetoric and troll culture endemic to today's far right, of Jean-Paul Sartre's famous dictum on anti-Semitism: "Never believe anti-Semites are completely unaware of the absurdity of their replies. They know that their remarks are frivolous, open to challenge. But they are amusing themselves."[16] It remains apt. But I've also often thought about the corollary implied by its conclusion: "It is [the anti-Semite's] adversary who is obliged to use words responsibly, since he believes in words." If indeed those opposed to fascism are obliged to use our words responsibly, can our belief in them be turned against us by our peers?

I think this is why we now so often litigate personal disputes with the lofty rhetoric of politics, because it *works* to shame and isolate those most like ourselves. To accept that you simply do not like someone is to accept something base and trivial, something that would be embarrassing to build a public campaign on by itself. But if you can accuse your hated rival of some political sin, some prejudice, some abuse, *then* it's worthy of a platform. One can marshal one's forces, confident in the attack. It'll be a just war.

It's hardly a "responsible" use of the language, but if you once accept that posting is, even potentially, praxis, it becomes trivially easy to convince yourself otherwise. Such politicization of personal differences lies at the heart of much fractiousness in revolutionary movements and other political communities united by the fragility of shared experiences of marginalization. It's so tempting because it offers the illusion of power — and you can well and truly hurt someone with it, deepening your hallucination of revolutionary strength. And when other avenues of power feel closed to you, when genuinely powerful people feel far away upon their fell Olympus, you may find yourself irresistibly tempted by the easy targets. You can lead yourself to believe that you've changed things, when all you've done is wound someone in a hopelessly interpersonal dispute.

No number of 911 Karens justly fired from their cubicle jobs will ever change or outweigh that fact.

***

The grotesque irony at the heart of Web 2.0 and the social media platforms that define it is that it is a profoundly individualistic space. Despite being sold as the pinnacle of collectivity, contemporary social media is the epitome of "together alone," the metropolis without the charm, mass society without the society. For all the power of social networking, bringing thousands or even millions of people together in ways that would've been impossible hitherto, it channels us only towards one another, individually, rather than towards any grand collective design.

Think about all of the social media campaigns you've gotten swept up in, or witnessed. Almost invariably the target was an individual; maybe, occasionally, a wealthy and powerful individual like a famous actor or author or columnist, but an individual all the same — some apparent symptom of a far larger problem, a far more insidious social illness. These platforms fling you at individuals. One more bad guy to knock down a peg. Sometimes, if you're very lucky, they even deserve it.

Yet what becomes clear, if you're honest with yourself, is that you're together alone with the mob. This isn't *really* a community, it isn't *really* a collective. It's a bunch of people crowdsourced into doing one thing to one person and then scattering back to the four winds when the deed is done. Even if that one person *deserved* the full weight of harassment, it's still pointillist justice at best. And this assumes everything else has gone right: that the target was well-chosen, the tactics ethically defensible, the outcome desirable. Rarely are all these conditions met.

Worse, there's no way to fix things if anything *does* go wrong — and it so frequently does. If some people are going too far in their abuse, you can't stop them. You'll likely just start meta-Discourse; the beat will drum on regardless. In point of fact, it'll probably be *helped* by your moral arguments, keeping the flames of attention stoked.

Sometimes, the outrage *about an outrage* keeps the flames lit. Consider a recent viral social media sensation that was all over the newspapers: the supposed TikTok trend about Osama bin Laden's "Letter to America," penned in 2002 to justify Al-Qaeda's attacks on 9/11. A handful of people on TikTok praised the anti-Semitic screed because it contained a few choice lines criticizing American empire. Repulsive as that is, it was just a few naïve idiots on TikTok. When journalist Yashar Ali assembled a supercut of a mere thirteen Tik-Toks on the matter, it turned into an international firestorm, with reports on television news and in newspapers all over the world. Ali did this — where else? — on Twitter, where all too many Extremely Online journalists hoovered it up. That, at last, caused the "Letter to America" nonsense to trend *genuinely*; it became the talk of social media.

I don't doubt that Ali's intentions were good, even if his motives were likely clouded by the kind of attention-seeking that ensnares us all on these platforms. But in amplifying this handful of Tik-Toks, he ended up creating a carnival of attention for reprehensible views that might otherwise have passed unremarked upon. So many social media paroxysms are like this. Even something truly objectionable, something that is the epitome of toxic social media — like an infamous case on

Twitter where a woman was harassed for expressing joy about having a "perfect morning" with her husband on the deck of their house drinking coffee because there were miserable people in the world who didn't know such joys — is dramatically amplified by *our recognition* of its toxicity. Everyone piles on, trying to bring justice to a manifestly unjust situation, but they succeed only in oxygenating the flames.

And for all that burning, smouldering risk, the reward is appallingly scant. Much as we'd prefer to think otherwise, all that pointillist justice doesn't add up to collective change, much less a revolution. Social media was always good at seducing us into thinking the trivial was important. Which can just be a benign misperception when we're talking about foodstagram or selfie trends or (especially) cat pictures. It becomes dangerous when we mistake the catharsis of callouts for actual justice or collective change.

But in an age when we're more online than ever — and where the pandemic made many of us even *more* dependent on social media than we already were in 2019 — we're mistaking a lot of what I've described here for the work of politics. Many people would've contended that they were doing good work during the harrowing of Isabel Fall. Instead, they only humiliated themselves and destroyed a life.

If that's what politics means to people, it's no wonder so many have come to regard it as a four-letter word.

Log Off

***

If it seems as though we've drifted a bit from the topic of shitposting, I'd contend that, on the contrary, we've gotten to its heart. The essence of shitposting lies in being entirely Too Online, in seeing it as an end in itself. That mentality can be bent towards an irony that removes you from even the *threat* of empathy — such that you can make the edgiest jokes about the biggest tragedies — or it can be bent towards the penance of weaponized sincerity, insisting that the internet is very serious business indeed and you are its (again, determinedly unempathetic) enforcer. This is why harassment campaigns of any sort are so often a mélange of humour and self-seriousness.

The humour takes the edge off, helps it feel a little less real, a little more hallucinatory. It also helps you make peace with the inherent point-lessness of it all. The call-outs that added up to so much less than the sum of their parts. The harassment that failed to fill the void you were shovelling it into. The hashtag campaigns that pushed awareness like Sisyphus's rock.

Shitposting could act as an immune sys-tem for the internet, per Ben Collins's suggestion, if two conditions were met: 1) that most of the targets of harassing shitposts actually deserved it; and 2) that harassing deserv-ing targets off platforms made a meaningful dif-ference to the user experience on each site.

Clearly enough, neither of these conditions are close to being met.

None of this is to say I don't *like* shitposting. Hell, my fiancée and I share shitposts and memes in bed together every morning, holding our phones up to each other's faces like little offerings of the most transient affection. One of my dearest friends and lovers delights in communicating with me through academic shitposts; another partner is the curator of my TikTok feed, sharing a homeostatic balance of shitpost Toks and earnest Toks. This is transfemme culture, and you can take it from my cold, shakily overcaffeinated hands. It is, as so many better nerds than I have pointed out, the realization of that *Next Generation* episode where the crew of the *Enterprise* meets a species that speaks entirely in metaphors and allegories. It's fun. It's hilarious. But it is not revolutionary.

It's too pat to say that the internet has made us too cool to care, even if that's marginally true. It's just not the whole story. We all care so much, so deeply. But on platforms like Twitter and its newfound legion of would-be successors, as well as on TikTok, or on older but still relevant platforms like Facebook, it remains too easy to lose all sense of how to deploy our most compassionate emotions with the requisite care. We can be left *scrambling* to care, as if suddenly shaken awake from a nightmare, and in our flailing and screaming we lash out against people like Isabel Fall — to say nothing of those many others whose names you either don't know or don't remember.

Of the many things the shitposting ethos and its effluence can be called, *political* is not one of them. We have to reckon with how this ethos's complete takeover of the culture of open social media platforms, these sorts of everyone-to-everyone platforms, has corroded not just our ability to care but also our ability to do so in a way that is measured and proportionate.

It's Not Your Fault You're an Asshole on Social Media

You ever see an argument on social media that makes you despise both sides with equal vigour? Or that makes you want to hurl yourself into one of those old McDonald's ball pits and slowly drown in cheap plastic?

There are obvious problems with giving specific examples of such poisonous interactions. For one thing, it would be ironic, given that my general purpose here is to gently urge you all to log off and stop paying attention to this sort of thing, if I directed too much of your attention towards it. It's also not entirely fair to the participants. On the other hand, it's hard, without a particular example of assholery, to really talk about where that assholery might be coming from.

So, as a sort of epigraph for this chapter, I want to start with a story about an exchange I recently witnessed on Bluesky, that touched off some Discourse.

Log Off

A trans woman comic artist skeeted:

> "Put Pronouns in Bio" put my dick in your throat *

A different trans woman (we'll call her Susan) then quote-skeeted:

> Holy shit white trans people are even more deranged here than on Twitter?!?!? This weirdo refuses to use tell people what their pronouns are because I guess we should know??? That's something else . . . . .
>
> oh they are also racist but that's largely a given ofc[†]

No additional context was given.

....

* The practice of putting pronouns in one's social media bio has never been uncontroversial; it's despised by right-wingers, for one thing, and a frequent source of outrage and derision for them. But it is now relatively mainstream among people who haven't made being a dick to trans folk their entire personality. And yet there's always been some discomfort around the sometimes coercive way in which introducing oneself through pronouns can take place. Some trans people feel singled out by it. Some don't like the idea strangers are entitled to some aspect of their gender identity. Some feel dysphoric from the implication that their preferred pronoun isn't obvious. This is what our comic artist was referencing, as lewdly as possible. Whether you agree with her or not is up to you, but try to disagree in a way that is... shall we say, more thoughtful than some of her interlocutors.

[†] Susan is also white. Earlier in this book, I noted that some users gleefully throw the eggshells on the ground that others feel compelled to tiptoe around, creating a perfect loop of toxic behaviour that involves white posters speaking above or for posters of colour. Here's a prime example.

This went over poorly with many Bluesky users, who immediately dogpiled Susan. One skeeted:

> I say this sincerely: If you keep digging you are going to hit a Main Character pipe. A rich vein of Main Character. You don't need to do this.

A true enough statement, and an apt reminder that Bluesky is merely a condensed version of Twitter — a point we'll return to presently.

The Art Decider account pronounced Susan's skeet:

> not art.

Someone rather aptly posted one of those Spider-men Pointing at Each Other memes. And then an argument started about whether the comic artist whom Susan targeted was actually white — a classic Discourse manoeuvre if ever there was one.

Finally, along came our epigraph, the *coup de grâce* that inspired this entire chapter. A man rolled up with this skeet, directed at Susan:

> You brought twitter toxicity into our new house of healing. The trans folx and slut coven are in charge here, and we are trying to keep this place welcoming and friendly. Disagreements are fine, but we don't quite dunk and we generally try to find the good. You did this to you. Put down the shovel 😊

Everyone then began dunking on *this* guy.

And, since I've now repeated this story — in a book, no less — I suppose I'm dunking on him too. For which action I can only humbly apologize to this man. I promise, it's not about you, it's about a vibe, an ideology, a system. Your words are merely a useful case study.

What's interesting about this skeet is that it epitomizes the idea that you can have Twitter But Good, Actually; that the novelty of the Twitter clones will allow us to start afresh, and somehow build a better, healthier social media platform. What this assumes is that we, as individuals, have significant power to influence the way these platforms develop. It's a kind of cybernetic wish-casting that's infected many users of the current crop of Twitter clones. It represents, above all, a profoundly and misguidedly individualistic understanding of platform culture.

* * *

There are two problems with most accounts of how social media works to produce certain kinds of behaviour in its users. Either 1) social media is treated as a cosmic idiot ball that entirely robs users of agency, hence all those "is social media making us dumber?" takes that periodically pepper newspapers; or 2) all problems on social media are ascribed to the moral defects of individuals. Despite seeming mutually exclusive, these errors are actually complementary and even symbiotic.

They're also eminently useful for a tech industry that thrives on self-mythologization. Either their product is omnipotent and influential (cue sluices of VC money) or the problems caused by their products are not their fault because PEBKAC — Problem Exists between Keyboard and Chair.

I never really accepted either perspective, even as I became more and more convinced that Web 2.0 social media really was increasingly bad for people's health and well-being, as well as increasingly deleterious for democracy itself. The problem wasn't with our private virtue, and it wasn't precisely because platforms make us into helpless automatons. There's give and take; we retain agency.

We are not, in short, simply plagued by morally defective people online. The notion that social media as it's currently constituted would be *wonderful* if we were all simply good little girls, boys, and enbies is attractive but fanciful. Aside from the obvious failings of any kind of "if everyone would *just do x*"-style argument (you can never make 100 percent of the population act a certain way 100 percent of the time), the truth is that the platforms we currently have are variously designed to foment crowds that bring out our inner asshole. We remain agents, responsible for our deeds, but it would be foolish to ignore how social media makes certain behaviours the path of least resistance — in every sense.

Some of you might've seen the examples of behaviour described in the previous chapter and thought, "I could never be like that," or "Yeah,

I hate *those people*." I myself fall prey to these thoughts constantly. And some people *are* just assholes on social media, just as they are in the physical world. But in my better moments I remember that the real problem is less with defective people than how these sites' systems guide us in particular directions.

To that end, having looked in depth at some of the problems that inhere in online culture on social media platforms, it's worth presenting a theory about what is making this beahviour so prevalent.

The viral nature of microblogging platforms is perfect for distilling those types of slapfights into a concentrated form and then, and this is key, *distributing* them. Sure, we saw this sort of thing on LiveJournal or on Usenet, but you had to go looking or get rather unlucky. Twitter and its various clones made it easy for such nonsense to get *everywhere*. Like sand.

***

Platform culture arises as a mélange of users and affordances. It is not merely the additive result of individual expressions, desires, or acts, but the multiplicative result of people acting in concert as they're swept along by the tides of social forces, as well as the way their environment conditions their behaviour.

To understand the latter, I want to elaborate on that word: *affordance*.

The term derives from the work of ecological psychologist James J. Gibson and his scholarship on direct perception.[17] Gibson defined an affordance as "what things furnish, for good or ill," particularly in reference to the environment in which an animal found itself. As with most seemingly simple academic terms, it took on a life of its own: wrangled over, disputed, used, reworked, and massaged into whatever neat shape suited the needs of a given researcher. One field in which that life is particularly vibrant has been technology studies.

As Sandra Evans, Katy Pearce, Jessica Vitak, and Jeffrey Treem (re)defined it, a specifically *technological* affordance must create "a link between an object and an outcome" *through* the affordance one is describing.[18] Thus a doorknob has the affordance of permitting a slight twisting motion to open a door; a handle has the affordance of allowing you to push down and pull in or push out to open the door; a push bar simply demands that you push. An affordance, in the simplest terms, is anything that allows you to do a specific thing. Colloquially, we might use terms like *feature* to describe it, or *gameplay* in a video game. These terms are imprecise, but they overlap a great deal with what actual affordances are. Push X, Y happens.

Jenny Davis took this one step further: she argued we should also ask *how* objects afford, rather than merely *what* they afford.[19] She defines affordances as "potentialities that operate in degrees through interactions with diverse subjects and circumstances," a very academic definition that serves some useful purposes.

Davis talks about the "mechanisms and conditions" of affordances.

"Mechanisms" are the *verbs* of affordance, e.g., does a given affordance in a piece of technology *demand* something of you or *prefer* it of you? When a website makes you change your password because it's out of date, that is a *demand*, an affordance that is connected to the outcome of account security. When a video game offers you medical kits to heal your character, it suggests that it *prefers* you use them, as the game is balanced around the assumption that you will. And so on.

Davis's "conditions," meanwhile, are the environments that affordances operate within (and, to a certain extent, create). That can be as literal as the design of a video game's open world of hills and valleys, helping structure the use of certain abilities, or as figurative as the way politics and power can make affordances *request* certain things of users while *demanding* them of others — e.g., if you're a remotely visible lefty trans woman online, using two-factor authentication is a requirement, not merely a nice-to-have. Online security matters more to some of us than others.

This brings me to the most important thing about affordances, which Davis understands and which is always worth flagging explicitly: affordances *condition* us. They shape our behaviour.

We learn what's possible, what's encouraged and discouraged, and we act accordingly. We turn the handle, and we open the door. We press X, and Y occurs.

How you behave on social media is the result of a mangle between your personal choices and morality, the platform affordances you have access to, and the social environment in which you find yourself. It's why you express yourself differently on different platforms. Instagram, Facebook, Discord, TikTok, and Twitter clones all *afford* different modes of engagement. Instagram compels visual expression; even as the text posts and comments remain important, the image is enthroned. The fact that the image is square also conditions *how* you "do it for the 'gram": you pre-frame your photos with the platform in mind. Meanwhile, Facebook and Discord permit more floridly textual interaction. Facebook can become like a blog, while Discord permits everything from rapid-fire chatroom nonsense to intense conversations between two people.

You have the potential for all this inside you, of course, but each platform moves you in different ways. They *request* and occasionally *demand* certain kinds of interactions. TikTok *demands* that you post something in the visual medium in order to use it, and *requests* shorter videos, for instance. Some of that is conditioned by what the platforms allow or disallow through their very code; some of that is conditioned by the subtler forces of rewarding certain behaviours over others.

Log Off

***

I can't tell you how many people I've heard from who remain wedded to various platforms even when they're in a mental health crisis that the platform is actively *worsening*, because "all my friends are there." Some of this is mere justification for an addiction, but it often has more than a little truth to it. People build rich social lives on certain platforms. Goddess knows I've met more than one girlfriend through Twitter, and there are still, in 2024, many people in my life with whom I only have substantial contact through Facebook: a dear friend working on her psych degree in Budapest, a theologian in Mississippi, a geologist in Maine, a game developer in Australia. I'd like to think we could work something out off the platform, but Facebook *affords* us an easy, low-impact way to update each other on our lives and stay in touch in a way that matters.

Affordances like this create a pulling effect that ties you to platforms, making migration or, dare one say, *logging off* challenging. The latter may even extract a monetary cost. But beyond pulling you back, the affordances, once you've logged on, also encourage particular kinds of use-patterns and behaviour.

Consider the affordances of a microblogging environment: the capacity to like, or to reply, or to repost, or to quote post. Think about the kinds of posts that are likely to do well (i.e., get likes and replies and reposts and quote posts) and so *go viral* in such an attention economy. Add in a wider environment where people frequently depend on visibility for some (or even all) of their income (Davis's "conditions" made manifest) and you have a recipe for some pretty ugly and awkward behaviour.

To wit, being argumentative, controversial, funny, or otherwise engaging are great ways to go viral and get attention. And often the kind of humour that gets privileged is at someone else's expense. It's not strictly your fault, of course. What are you going to do? Starve? You need to get attention. You need a following. You need eyeballs on your Twitch stream. Customers in your Etsy shop. Players for your game. (Readers for your argumentative book-length essay on logging off.)

Or perhaps you only *hope* you get attention. Most of us don't *have* to pursue or participate in virality, of course. It's just *requested* of us. Frequently. Especially if large parts of our social life are also channelled through a given platform. Even if we have nothing to sell, we quickly grasp that there are pleasurable, intangible rewards for being noticed.

The quote-tweet is an especially useful example of this. For some, the quote-tweet is a sword of justice; for others, it's a Sword of Damocles. A tool for righteous callouts, or a tool for harassment — two ways of saying the same thing, some might argue. I wouldn't, myself. Sometimes you *do* need a quote-tweet to drop a truth bomb on a deserving target. And of course, it has more salubrious uses as well. I've often used it to "yes, and" the words of dear friends and colleagues who said something interesting or clever. In every event, it permits and conditions interaction. It makes certain types of abuse easier by pinning a target to one's timeline, but it also facilitates constructive sharing and amplification. It permits commentary.

Which, of course, brings us back to the quote-skeets that sent us on this merry adventure through the wonderful world of affordances.

***

What affordances mean, I've argued, is that you cannot act just as you please — you're bound by your environment, the terms of service, the platform's design, even the behaviour of others. You may find yourself unwilling to express yourself in a certain way if you think it'll have less than desirable outcomes, or meet with the opprobrium of your fellow users.

It's worth rereading Mr. Good Vibes Only in that light: "You brought twitter toxicity into our new house of healing" is an incredibly cringeworthy way to describe Bluesky, which is not so much a house of healing as a halfway house for Twitter addicts unable to go cold turkey. "The trans folx and slut coven are in charge here, and we are trying to keep this place welcoming and friendly." No, no we are not. This is incredibly disingenuous and even dangerous. "Disagreements are fine, but we don't quite [*sic*] dunk and we generally try to find the good." One wonders if this person used Bluesky for more than five minutes.

Why am I fisking this skeet to death* if I'm *also* railing against Twitter toxicity hard enough to write a book about it? Because it presents a theory of the case so compelling it has many adherents on the various platforms people scattered to in hopes of replacing Twitter's violently costly dopamine hits. We just need to "be kind," and practise mindfulness and project good vibes. If enough of us do that, we'll fix the platform's culture!

The delusion that Bluesky has been taken over by us trannies and sluts is more than a little rich. Admittedly, a cadre of lefty trans shitposters and a non-trivial group of sex workers have both built significant presences on Bluesky — at least, as of this writing — but they own nothing. The people who actually own and run the platform are predominantly cisgender and certainly aren't sex workers. Power, then, does not truly reside with the trannies and sluts. They won't even act collectively most days, the one source of a sliver of power they do have. Even when they do, it is unlikely to change the trajectory of the platform in meaningful ways. Cosmetic changes, sure. Little tweaks to the Terms of Service? Perhaps.

One trans poster has even made a name for herself as a volunteer moderator of sorts, using her combined mute-lists as a kind of crowdsourced means

....

* Another one for the "phrases I never thought I'd string together" bucket.

of helping to police the site of bad actors. In a word, she's giving Bluesky free labour — useful labour that's earned her the gratitude of many users as it helps improve their experience. But it's not ownership. Nor is it meaningful control. It's an attempt to use the affordances of the platform in ways that benefit some of its more marginalized users. For now, Bluesky doesn't disapprove of this use case. It may not always be so.

As Bluesky grows, will it continue to be a tolerant place for sex workers to both ply their trade and simply exist openly without fear? I doubt it. There's absolutely no reason to believe that the old cycle of profiting from sex workers when the platform is young while banning them after mainstream acceptance of the platform is assured has been broken here. If Bluesky thinks they need to crack down on sex work to secure capital or operate in certain territories, no amount of hashtagging will stop this.

This myth, that power rests with the users, has always proven useful to social media's corporate overlords. That's why it's called YouTube, not BoardOfDirectorsTube. Myths like the one put around by Mr. Good Vibes Only help obfuscate the ways that corporate power works, and the fact that platforms are designed first and foremost as profit-generating machines, which extract value from us by dint of our very presence.

***

As for Susan... Mr. Good Vibes Only thinks Susan is *individually* the problem, that making a platform better is simply a matter of ensuring that individuals behave themselves better. What he's not asking is why Susan's shtick works so well so often for so many people.

Now, perhaps Susan really is an asshole, online and off. Perhaps she was knowingly exploiting controversy for clout. Perhaps she was being performative and cruel in a pointless argument about arguments in a bid for attention. This might be true. It's certainly true that she used the ensuing outrage about her quote-skeet to create content, even going so far as to market herself as the "#1 BLOCKED BSKY USER." But who knows, perhaps, for some ill-defined reason, she really believed that her target was a racist, and that this skeet was the optimal way of dealing with that problem.

The key point here, however, the thing Mr. Good Vibes Only completely misses, is that, whether calculatingly or not, Susan was operating on a program that has repeatedly been proven effective: enter a platform with a bucket of shit and stir vigorously, then bask in that sweet, sweet engagement as everyone starts complaining about the bad smell. Be controversial, pick fights, acquire currency — or, at least, attention that you might be able to redeem for currency later, as with the Pepsi Points of old. And of course, just like Pepsi Points, it's all a corporate scam dressed up as empowerment.

What's clear is that Susan could be anybody. She's not unique. If it wasn't her, it would've been someone else. Someone will stir shit, and because of the design of the platform, they *will* get attention. Susan got dunked on aplenty, along with a bit of harassment to boot. She quickly became the target of a blocking campaign. But people who do what Susan did won't stop coming to Bluesky. Indeed, many of the people who harangued her will make a post like hers when they think it's justified, when they think they've got the *right* target in their sights.

The vast networked exposure of all of us to one another, without significant filtering, allowing everyone to talk to everyone simultaneously, often has an effect on Discourse. You start performing for an audience. And while there *is* such a thing as bad publicity online, you can still frequently parlay even bad publicity into something worthwhile. In the immortal words of Oscar Wilde, there is only one thing in life worse than being talked about, and that is not being talked about.

***

The basic structures of the platform then — its affordances — make being an asshole easy and even desirable, while they make genuine social change harder. In a case study such as this, there's no choice but for the court to exonerate all the individuals involved; each was dancing to a tune set long before they'd logged in that day. One harassed for the sake of building social capital, another wishcast about power he didn't truly have in order to feel good about his chosen platform.

But what about *you*, dear reader? Perhaps, by this point, you've started to think more critically about some of the things you've said and done online? Perhaps you're wondering — despite all we've discussed so far — if *you're* a bad person. "Sure, maybe Susan's behaviour can be analyzed out of all ethical implication, but not *me*. I'm built different. I'm worse."

And perhaps you *have* done regrettable things. Perhaps you've been swept up in some kind of online harassment campaign, responding to the call when someone quote-tweeted some jackass or "problematic" individual, chipping in with a witty retort, a meme, a cutting barb. How can we better understand why you might've done that, despite your ethics? What if you put this book down right now and ended up getting swept up in such a campaign anyway, even with my pretentious nagging still ringing in your ears? As we've been discussing, there's a lot that's beyond your control.

Well, do I have some academic therapy for you! Let's do an anatomy of a harassment campaign together.

***

I'm used to comics breaking my heart; I'm a *The Wicked + The Divine* fan, after all. But I felt the particularly painful crack of an old fissure reopening as I read cartoonist Mallorie Udischas-Trojan's "Piled On" at the *Nib*. It described the pain of being, in her words, "on the other side of an online hatefest." It begins with a jokey comic she wrote in April 2020 in which a character shoplifted supplies from an art store. The point of that comic was that the character shoplifted tons of art supplies to break her artist's block and yet still couldn't figure out what to draw. Simple, silly, and fun.

But, of course, Twitter did as Twitter does.

A firestorm ensued on the platform, which saw Udischas-Trojan accused of valorizing "crime," promoting anti-worker practices (shoplifting gets employees into trouble, and because of this, one should be furious at shoplifters and comic artists who depict them rather than at corporations, for some reason), and just generally being over-privileged, flippant, or otherwise unworthy of participating in public Discourse. Though it began with transphobes and right wingers attacking her, there were many "concerned" friends and allies who also thought she'd gone too far.

"Piled On," posted at the end of 2021, is an insightful autobiographical account this experience that, and, especially, of what the betrayal by online friends — the vaunted "community" we all seek from social media — meant to her.

The tenth panel of "Piled On" is what really caused my heart to shatter. It depicted Udischas-Trojan's own heartbreak at friends and allies joining the dogpile. The speech bubble next to her self-portrait, which read "I . . . I really thought we were rooting for each other," just about broke me. I've been there, and I have many friends and colleagues who've experienced their own versions of this sort of lateral abuse. You yourself may well have known some version of this.

Many seem to imagine that a greater focus on personal responsibility can detoxify the internet; surely Udischas-Trojan's progressive harassers, her erstwhile friends, were just bad people all along? I myself promoted the idea of digital ethical education as part of the solution to problems like these. One of my more widely cited academic papers, entitled "Ethics for Cyborgs," argues that gamers — the population my paper focused on — will need to engage in a "process of ethical discovery" that would involve them "thinking critically about the values that they hold, what they truly believe about each other, their hobby, the space they inhabit, and what play truly means for them." While I also proposed other solutions to harassment — changing the design of games, improved moderation practices — a lot of what I called for was oriented towards earnestly and consciously encouraging users to behave better.

Alas, the tragic reality is that our good intentions — in whichever direction they may run — are so easily twisted online, corrupted from their purpose by forces beyond our control. The affordances of particular social media platforms, which we discussed earlier, are a huge part of that equation. But the internet as a whole has affordances of its own: as a distributed network, it affords us the ability to harass and harm people without ever once interacting with them directly. Your intent is irrelevant. Even, crucially, if it's an attempt to *defend* the person being harassed.

In the end, online harassment campaigns twist questions of personal responsibility and virtue into strange shapes, or even renders them immaterial. A campaign needs individuals to participate, but, as with Agatha Christie's murderers on the Orient Express, no one knows who in the crowd strikes the fatal blow.

***

In my academic research, I've tried to give analytic rigour to the idea of a "harassment campaign," identifying it as possessing three qualities social media is designed to cultivate almost automatically: crowdsourcing, organization, and longevity. The campaign against Udischas-Trojan was originated, and even organized to an extent, by certain individuals, but the platform did most of the work, rapidly crowdsourcing like-minded people to like, retweet, and contribute their two cents to the drama. And, of course, it *lasted*. It went on for days and weeks at a time.

What sustains such a campaign is a structure that can best be visualized as an inverted pyramid, bearing down on an often helpless individual target, in descending degrees of severity. What I term first- and second-order harassment is the abuse you're most likely familiar with, from the violence of swatting someone to the casual cruelty of abusing someone through a tweet or email or TikTok directed at them.

But it's the third order that gets at what this chapter has really been about. This third order is not hacking the target or engaging with them to spew abuse. Rather, it describes the simple act of *commenting* on the situation. In the case of the harassment of Udischas-Trojan, people who were lamenting the act of "promoting shoplifting" or otherwise Discoursing *about* the practice would've been engaging in this third-order harassment. It is, in sum, the enabling, apologism, and justificatory Discourse about the target that ensures most people participating feel as if they're doing the right thing that makes more overt and intense forms of harassment possible:

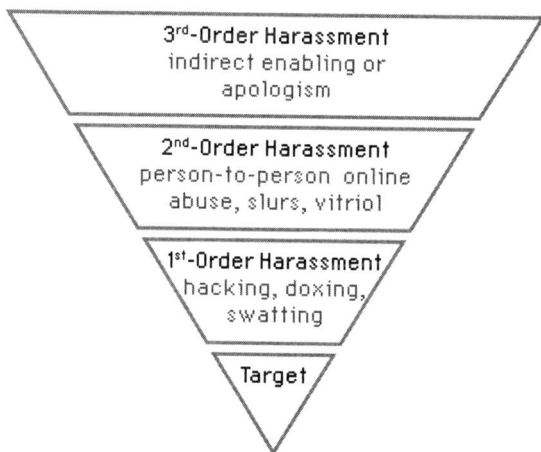

3rd-Order Harassment
indirect enabling or apologism

2nd-Order Harassment
person-to-person online abuse, slurs, vitriol

1st-Order Harassment
hacking, doxing, swatting

Target

Crucially, third-order behaviour exceeds private intentions. Most of the people in this tier don't intend to do harm. From high-minded pseudo-philosophizing to a mocking Tok to ironizing on Twitter, any Discourse *about* the target keeps them foremost in the hive mind. If there's no such thing as bad publicity, there's also no such thing as *good* social media Discourse once you've become a Main Character.

When we talk about Discourse with a capital *D*, this is often what we mean. We're referring to discussions that orbit a specific person, even if they're not directly referenced, linked to the conversation, or tagged into it. This is also what happened to Isabel Fall. All the online abuse that nearly claimed her life was in some sense third order. No one had a social media handle or email to send abuse *to*, after all. Indeed, this simple fact about her itself became part of the the Discourse. It helped justify the suspicion that lent fire to all the abuse: if she wasn't Logged On, she *had* to be a Nazi cat's paw, a fiction, some sock puppet or troll. Yet she did, nevertheless, see and experience the worst of the worst. And it all sustained the climate that heaped that pain on her, that justified it and demanded more.

In Udischas-Trojan's case, the moral rationales for attacking her — people who argued that her comic was a "bad take" or that it painted artists in a bad light or that shoplifting "actually hurts workers" — weren't directed *at* her; they just served to *justify* further discourse and rationalize the furor over a completely innocent comic. The target may not see third-order discourse, but they'll certainly feel its effects.

"Where there's smoke, there's fire," we often say, to justify suspicion and a presumption of guilt. Third-order harassment is a smoke machine.

***

When I explain to students how a video game's or social media platform's design may contribute to anti-social behaviour, my go-to metaphor is road design. Road design in countries like the Netherlands promotes what is known as "traffic calming." For instance, roads narrow gradually into streets to force cars to slow down, streets themselves are narrower, speed bumps are more common — even crosswalks are raised to produce a speed bump effect where the most lives might be saved. And save lives this road design has: when all the elements are taken together, it's reduced pedestrian deaths and car accidents alike. By contrast, road design in North America often promotes high-speed driving, passively nudging drivers to step on the gas, giving them less time to stop, even in crowded areas.

By thinking about design, you can get away from solely individualist narratives about accidents — about bad drivers or "pedestrians who weren't looking" — and focus on how the affordances of the system we find ourselves within encourage broad outcomes not attributable to any one actor.

111

Like North American roads, social media is designed in a way that agitates, rather than calms, its traffic. It leans into, rather than away from, the augmented reality aspects of computer use — tricking us into believing we're somewhere other than reality.*

Nearly all internet use is fundamentally dissociative, subtly divorcing us from the consequences of our words and deeds. There's a seductive quality to posting into the void, a Möbius-strip sense that you're at once the voyeur whom no one *can* see and the exhibitionist whom everyone *must* see. Psychologist John Suler dubbed this the "dissociative imagination." In my own research, I came to this conclusion from the other direction, arguing that in online *gaming* spaces, the magic circle conceit of video gaming enabled people to extend the game's unreality to their own words and actions. But I eventually realized that it wasn't just games that had this effect; it was the entire online space, disinhibiting and ludic all at once.

Like most structural problems, from the ongoing pandemic to climate change to the rampant

....

* On most open platforms, there are relatively few speed bumps between a post and its effect, especially if it goes viral. Consider the way a single tweet can become quote-tweeted and/or dogpiled, for instance, with few limitations beyond locking one's account. As I note elsewhere, Bluesky actually does some good here by installing a speed bump. When you block a user, it's cauterizing: their posts disappear from your thread, and neither's quote-skeets can appear to the other's followers. This genuinely cuts off a vector of possible harassment. But, even so, the platform remains broadly open, and, like Twitter, when Discourse catches fire, it burns like a forest in a late Anthropocene summer.

inequalities that worsen the devastation of both, we cannot delude ourselves into believing that additive individual virtue will be enough to overcome the problem — especially when people commenting on every side *feel* virtuous.

That doesn't mean you have no responsibility when using social media, of course. In both the Helicopter Story and the Shoplifting Comic Saga, many progressives who went on the attack were picking up on rumours started by right-wing harassers spreading deliberate disinformation. Abandoning the "where there's smoke, there's fire" mentality we all have about internet callouts can only serve us well.

But sometimes there's simply nothing to say that *won't* cause trouble, which is one of many reasons why the periodic appearance of think pieces about Twitter discourse masquerading as dispatches from the front line of "the Culture War" is risible.* The idea there is some cabal of lefty Twitter power users convening at a summit to set the right level of ironic vitriol for their tweets, as if setting oil production quotas at OPEC, has always been absurd.

The problem isn't that a given platform's *users* are toxic, it's that the platform makes toxicity the path of least resistance, and turns even intetionally positive commentary into just more fuel

....

* Consider Jesse Singal's four-part (yes, four-part) Substack series entitled "YA Twitter's Victims and Critics Speak Out." There are few phrases so cursed in our language as "four-part Substack series about YA Twitter," but it certainly paints a picture.

for the fire. This is what the road design of social media has wrought: like a wide, straight road encouraging dangerous speeding, the limitless void of social media encourages pained shouting, and its financially backed incentive structures make an addicting game out of the whole affair.

So no, it's not your fault you get twisted to nastiness on social media. But if that corruption is inexorable, there are some uncomfortable implications. Not least that these platforms, supposedly all about you and allowing you to broadcast your truest self to the world, don't give a damn about your good intentions.

***

Solutions are few and far between. We have already discussed the ineffectiveness of individualistic remedies. Perhaps *you* can simply avoid participating in the Discourse of the day — even if that feels tantamount to self-censorship and/or deprives one of the social networks and career opportunities these platforms readily provide. But it won't change the way the whole platform operates.

Structural-level solutions are often even worse. Involving the police will simply redouble *other* problems, disproportionately punishing the poor and powerless. Paeans to "inclusiveness", on the other hand, will come to nothing, at best finding more progressive ways of phrasing existing policies and designs. Purely technical solutions, finally, merely tinker around the edges, or dull our ability to hear the crowd, rather than actually calming the noise emanating from it.

If we had built the internet around the idea of our embodied humanity, rather than the naive idea that we should be *liberated* from it, dissociation might not have come so easily. Early on, we configured the internet as a place that automatically freed us from the burdens of our identities — race, religion, gender, disability; none of it seemed to matter online, where, in the words of a famous *New Yorker* cartoon, no one knows you're a dog. The very metaphor of cyberspace as an alternative universe we teleport into, shedding the coils of identity that bind us "in real life," reinforced this, and it is partly to blame here. But that ship has well and truly sailed, in any event. We remain stuck on platforms that we depend on, even as they impel us towards nasty, or even cruel, behaviour.

Worst of all, however, is the way this puts the lie to the idea of community online. So many of the things that social media supposedly does well, the various attributes that might stack the Pros column in its favour, turn out to be heavily qualified; sometimes they're even Cons. If the community you seek online vituperates you and bullies you because they just happened to get swept up in the day's Discourse, because they're so vulnerable to the clockwork of social media affordances grinding away their good intentions, then was it really a community at all? When everything you put out into the ether of an open platform could be harmful, despite your most dearly felt wishes and intentions, you have to ask yourself whether it's really worth it to post on that day.

But what if you log off to an empty room that stays empty? Well, that's where we come to the idea of a more decentralized internet. Before the current age of social media, I made plenty of friends and found community through everything from online games like *Neverwinter Nights* or *World of Warcraft*, to forums, to chat protocols like IRC. Today's equivalents, like Discord, remain better places to form something that more closely resembles a community.

The best part about a more cellular strategy for maintaining a high-quality personal network is that it's a form of what we might call web-traffic calming. Drama and dissociation remain inevitable — the internet is still the internet — but their impacts will be much more closely contained. It's easier for you to seal off a chatroom, or boot a single toxic user from it, than to single-handedly clean up all of Twitter or Tumblr or Bluesky or TikTok. In this way, you can reclaim one of the most oversold benefits of social media — that of community — and make it something meaningful.

The open nature of major platforms — open to the entire world — is a real benefit, yes. But it's worth remembering that you're clamouring for attention *along with* all those other people. Even if you earn yourself thousands of followers, the engagement they're likely to give you is minimal. On Twitter, even when I had 27,000 followers, it was a rare day when something I tweeted got over 50 retweets. Fundraising appeals — one of the more important things that people say they need social media for — were *very* hard to propel, no matter how hard I tried to leverage an audience the size of a small city. It still did something, of course, just far less than you'd think, given the sheer numbers involved.

In the same way, smaller, more focused platforms may give you lower engagement figures, but each dollop of engagement — each like, each share, each comment — is more apt to *mean* something. That higher-quality engagement has a better chance of giving you a real sense of community, furnishing you with real people you can depend on, who will have your back and who, because they're closer to you — digitally and personally — will be better equipped to stay out of any sudden mobs that get spun up by open social media. And it's also less likely to make you behave like an asshole.

Yes, there will still be drama and hell to pay sometimes. I'm a LiveJournal lass, and I remember the theatrics far better than I should. But you'll be able to contain it better, and you'll be in a position to select your friends — your *real* friends — more easily. Community is not something you simply find waiting for you on a platform like Twitter or Bluesky. One way or another, you have to build it.

The Oubliette of Terror

"The only thing we have to fear is fear itself." This is a line burned into the memory of anyone with even a passing acquaintance with American history — one you could almost certainly parody with a cheeky imitation of FDR's voice, with its stentorian mid-Atlantic accent. The line is from his first inaugural address, in 1933. But the full sentence has more to offer than the catchy opening clause: "The only thing we have to fear is fear itself — *nameless, unreasoning, unjustified terror which paralyzes needed efforts to convert retreat into advance.*" That last bit is the kicker; it turns a pithy bon mot into an *argument*.

"The only thing we have to fear is fear itself," taken out of context as a general statement, is easy enough to cavil at; there is, in fact, much in the world worth being afraid of. But the full idea articulated by FDR is not so easy to dismiss with pedantry. The thesis of this speech is a lesson about democracy, too often forgotten on those occasions where fear is *most* justified, like the Great

Depression of which Roosevelt spoke. The real danger of unchecked fear is that it becomes "nameless, unreasoning terror" that "paralyzes" true political action — the very thing that might *address* the source of our fears.

Things are undeniably, catastrophically awful right now. We're confronted with widespread challenges to the very idea of democracy, the world is burning, we've limped bleeding from a deadly pandemic, inflation has mobilized the vegetable aisle against us, and now the fascists are trying to kill us. Even this pithy summary seems barely to scratch the surface. In the midst of these real reasons to be afraid, however, social media makes us hyper-aware of everything going on in a way that seems designed to engender paralysis, and leave us all trapped in our own individualized oubliettes of terror.

***

Social media platforms amplify minoritarian voices — a potential virtue when looked at from the perspective of the truly marginalized and oppressed, but an obvious vice when considered from a perspective of disinformation and abuse. Or despair. Imagine you write a tweet and you receive twenty replies, all negative and cruel. You'd understandably feel quite miserable and, perhaps, like the whole world was mad at you. You could, of course, remind yourself that it was twenty people out of a platform that has hundreds of thousands of active users, in a nation of hundreds of millions. Whatever happened there, you could rightly tell yourself, it's not a scientific poll. But it's extraordinarily hard to maintain that level of awareness and equanimity, especially about hostile content.

Hostility is hard enough to deal with when it involves personal beefs that pervade open social media — being called out for something you didn't do, insulted cruelly for something you *did*, or just getting pointlessly wrapped up in misleading accounts of other people's drama. The effect can be to make you feel needlessly terrible. But what happens when you combine this effect with truly lofty political events and use the pinhole of social media to gaze at the world-historical? The answer is that a similar effect obtains on open platforms when it comes to bad news that feeds our terror: even true stories, amplified, may distort our sense of how representative they are.

The COVID pandemic illustrated this clearly. There were, obviously, very good reasons to fear COVID. But social media helped us dwell in "nameless, unreasoning terror" in the face of the disease. Paralyzed by stay-at-home orders and lockdowns, fearing a truly deadly and devastating disease with no cure, and stuck in front of our computers, those who were *able* to stay at home could subsist only on a steady diet of truly awful news. So, we dwelt in the fear. It provided the illusion of knowledge and control, and we sought as many renewable sources of it as possible. That included lingering luridly over anecdotes of trauma, death, and terminal illness. Is it any wonder some scammers were drawn to the prospect of so many likes and retweets?

I recall seeing more than one tale fly around Twitter about a "young, healthy person" who caught COVID four times before finally dying of a stroke. This tale was then used by various posters to suggest everything from 1) vaccines don't work as well as advertised (a point stressed by the "I believe in science" crowd almost as assiduously as the anti-vaxxers), to 2) the disease's impacts are being understated by the government and everything is much worse than we're "being told," to 3) such a case is not only real, but *representative*. Even the most robust statistics, however, do not bear out number 3; such cases, if real, remained extreme outliers. They did not paint an accurate picture of the modal experience of the disease for most people, even the medically vulnerable.

It was a struggle for me as a woman living with asthma to find accurate information about my risk profile. I knew I was *at risk*, but *how much*? I eventually stopped relying on anecdotes and focused on academic research or reliable interpretations thereof by experts. What good did it do me to try to map my experience and risk profile onto a twenty-three-year-old with asthma who died or got long COVID, as described on Twitter, who may or may not have even existed?

Consider the case of BethAnn McLaughlin, who tweeted under the pseudonym @Sciencing_Bi. Not only was she a white woman pretending to be

Native American, but she also feigned having long COVID and even faked her own death from the disease, taking advantage of the goodwill of many scientists she was networked with in progressive groups on social media. Then there's the case of the scholar Robert Honeyman, who claimed they lost their sister to COVID-19 and that their husband was put into a coma by the disease. Neither of those people were real. According to the *Daily Beast's* exposé on the matter, "Honeyman's main topic of online discussion was how the deadly pandemic was ongoing and nobody seemed to be paying attention." Reporters Pilar Melendez and William Bredderman added:

> Five days later, the user tweeted that their sister was put on a ventilator after being diagnosed with COVID — claiming that "she didn't believe COVID was a serious [*sic*] and didn't take precautious." [*sic*] On Nov. 12, Honeyman went viral after revealing their sister had "passed away from covid."

It's an unfortunate pattern, trading on the familiar tropes of hectoring and shaming around COVID that came to take over left-of-centre Twitter. Exaggerations and scams that prey on our worst fears are commonplace enough on social media, but precious little thought is given to how they might contribute to distorting our larger picture of truly important events. Worse, these misrepresentations undermine the utility of these platforms when they are trying to get *genuine* stories out. There are people sharing their struggles with long COVID or their grief over lost loved ones who do not deserve to have aspersions cast on them because of the perfidy of these sorts of fakers — any more than people of colour deserve to have aspersions cast on our identities because of people like McLaughlin.*

But it remains worth reflecting on how these frauds affect our sense of things and why they feel incentivized to go this route in the first place. Whatever the personal reasons, in each case, for their cyber-Münchausen's-syndrome, they do this because it works: because there's a real hunger for bad news, for the repetitive motion of self-harm represented by doomscrolling through this sort of thing.

✳✳✳

So, what do I find myself doomscrolling for? Sometimes, it's the escalating assault in the US and abroad on trans people's right to exist in public, or at all. And with good reason: the picture is grim.

....

* And let me tell you, as a light-skinned Latina whose heritage has been the subject of unkind speculation online, I have *thoughts* about white people consciously pretending not to be so. The hammer falls hardest on the great many of us whose racial identities are more "ambiguous," and who deal with doubt about that fact from both our own people and whites. Among the many other things social media enables, it makes life easier than ever for these scammers, and it also facilitates a similarly toxic counter-movement claiming to root out pretenders, which invariably catches many innocent people in the dragnet.

Online and in the media, we are simultaneously scapegoated for the endurance of patriarchy and libelled as "groomers" or pedophiles; CPAC speakers call to "eradicate transgenderism," demanding that every trans person should detransition on pain of some as yet undisclosed punishment; across the US, laws are being put forward, and enacted, that criminalize trans children and rob them of health care, ban us from public accommodations, and even threaten the health care of transgender adults; angry men with guns increasingly feel empowered to turn up at any public library where a drag queen is reading to kids. In Tennessee, they even passed a ban on drag performances that is so vaguely written that it could easily be taken to apply to any gender-nonconforming person who performs or even speaks in public — which was doubtless the intention. Even as these laws are challenged or struck down in courts, they send a signal, crowdsourcing garden-variety prejudice and sowing confusion about trans people.

No one should doubt the depth of the threat this entails to *everyone's* rights, and only a Pollyanna could even hope to pretend that everything is fine right now. But there are also plenty of reasons to have hope. If we look around at our offline lives, we know this. Online, however, the panoptic ubiquity of bad news and worse takes can create an illusion of inevitable doom for those already living under threat, closing off any hope of a life *worth* living — a world where a Fourth Reich is inevitable, the ineluctable resolution to an equation written long ago. I see so many of my fellow trans people torn apart by the anguish and loneliness of the Doomscroll; the algorithms of social media bloodlessly feed that despair, creating a feedback loop.

Positivity culture — all that "good vibes only" nonsense — is deeply toxic in its own right, as I've already argued above. But that essential truth is often used to imply that illimitable negativity is both Right and True. For marginalized groups, the latter point of view often becomes a licence to wallow in our own misery and fear, even as we keep telling ourselves that such a bacchanal of terror is good and healthy. And in doing so, we play right into the hands of the very people who hate us.

It's not uncommon to hear some jumped-up podcaster on a far-right blog feign concern over trans people's "self-mutilation" and suicide rate — the infamous 41 percent rate of attempted suicide among trans people. In a sickening repudiation of the idea that dwelling on ugly details is somehow helpful to us, that number is now used to harass us. Sometimes, some forum-dweller pops up on a trans person's social media and tells them simply "41%"; or, in the truly nasty places where harassment campaigns are organized, some users express a wish for an especially hated trans woman to "join the 41%." When we dwell on our suffering, we're not abjuring the lies of our oppressors; we're wallowing in their fantasies.

Log Off

Sociologist Laurel Westbrook calls this state of unending terror, the sense of infinite vulnerability and futility, "an unlivable life." They draw from the work of many other scholars in their examination of trans activist materials from 1990 to 2009, the long dawn of the transgender rights movement, and argue that their hyper-focus on extravagantly gruesome murders — like the killings of Brandon Teena and Gwen Araujo — had the unintended consequence of teaching a generation of trans people that our lives were permanently endangered and unlivable. But a livable life requires more than an awareness of threats. The minimization of joy, Westbrook argues, leaves transgender people terrified and, worse, "these narratives do not push people to stand up against the violence so much as run away and hide." There are, then, very real pitfalls to even well-intentioned emphases on threats. Indeed, hyper-awareness of threats can represent a threat all on its own. And hyper-awareness is all that many social media platforms offer.

***

Falling into the oubliette of terror has always been a risk on Twitter. It's exponentially worse now that Twitter isn't even pretending to moderate or control bigotry. I saw so many complaints from people about the new "For You" tab on the Twitter timeline when it was deployed in mid-2023; countless people reported an extraordinary amount of far-right bigotry being suggested to them.

This didn't happen to everyone. In fact, at the time — my last days on Twitter, admittedly — the far-right onslaught I feared didn't quite materialize in my own timeline. Part of that likely has to do with the fact that I wasn't asking the platform to show it to me. But others may unthinkingly doomscroll their way into telling Twitter's algorithm to show them ever more exotic sources of misery — particularly by interacting with, commenting on, or quote-tweeting to dunk on bigoted posts or bad news.

The issue is that social media is personalized. Social media, even as it turns *you* into a product, *is* a product in its own right. It can only ever be designed to offer *you* something — some devil's bargain in exchange for your money or your time or a bit of your soul in the form of endless selfies, something for *you*, and only *you*, in all your exquisitely unique needs and desires. Mercury that perfectly moulds itself to your contours, curves, and scars.

Most social media algorithms are not, truth be told, terribly mysterious. They rely on fairly simple signals: What do you interact with the most, what do you pay attention to, how long did you watch that video? In short, they're optimized for attention; whatever we get stuck on, the platform then gives us more of the same.

If we pay attention to people who hate us, even to argue with or mock them, the algorithm gives us more of them. Doomscrolling, quote-dunking, the obsessive fixation on what the most awful people on a platform are saying, will all end up serving you more of the same, entrenching these behaviours and starting a ceaselessly vicious cycle. And with mechanical remorselessness, the algorithms target the most vulnerable the hardest. When that happens, the suffocating excesses of far-right transphobic content can become truly overwhelming.

Musk may have made it worse. By removing any restriction on transphobic speech, *and* inviting back hordes of previously banned Nazis, TERFs, and other assorted bigots, he may have further inflated their already artificial sense of ubiquity, making them seem even louder and more numerous. But even *this* distortion effect is merely layered atop the existing distortions of this form of social media, where a handful of people can manipulate virality to seem more popular, more representative than they really are.

Twitter has always been terrible, but all this is not just a problem there; it is true of any Twitter clone, or TikTok, or any other similarly designed open platform. Whatever dropped-vowel nonsense has become the Next Big Thing by the time this book is in your hands will likely be designed along similarly exploitable principles.

Open platforms allow bad news and the bigots who thrive on it to loom as large as possible — shadow puppets climbing high on the walls of our minds in the shapes of towering monsters. In this way, social media algorithms lead us all to believe that our life will be impossible, that organizing or resisting will be impossible, that the only route is despair. Worse yet, we're staring into this pit of despair and ennobling this act of self-harm with a sense of duty.

***

Social media doens't just show us reasons to despar, either. Crucially, it shows us each other *living* in despair too.

Here's how it goes: First you doomscroll and become terrified, then you vent. You're in pain, dammit. Because of the structure of the internet, it probably feels as though you're shouting into the compliant void, the digital equivalent of screaming into a pillow. Perhaps you'll be validated by others who will remind you that you are worthwhile. Or perhaps you'll just find people you can yell at to make yourself feel better. Either way, that's restoration, you can express yourself freely, without the faintest hint of censorship, and feel just a bit better. But who hears you?

The fantasy being sold by these platforms is that *you* are the centre of everything, and vast quantities of money are sloshed around making that fantasy feel true. Consider every TikTok user who's gawked at the supposed eeriness of that platform's algorithm and how it seems to "know" them, or the way Facebook serves you ads related to a conversation you had with a friend two hours earlier. The net effect of marketing a product built around *you* is to individualize every user.

Under such circumstances, one's obligation to a larger community dissolves; your search for catharsis, your anxiety, your need to soothe your emotional state in the precise way that works for you, takes precedence over all else. You have a *right* to "take up space," to engage in self-care, to put your own needs first, et cetera. We can politicize this; we can say that we as women are socialized to put ourselves last, so there's something emancipatory about all this. Or perhaps you feel that your voice as a person of colour, or a queer person, or a fat person is stilled by societal demands and ugly stereotypes. Now you can be loud and proud. It isn't just self-care anymore, it's *politics*.

On an open platform, there's no way to make that work without every cheap-as-free dream intruding on every other. Hence, every conflict that you've seen: someone's catharsis is someone else's harassment; someone's release is someone else's grief; someone's self-expression is someone else's importuning. In the process, our endless misery may serve only to feed everyone *else's*.

To point this out is not victim blaming. You didn't do this to yourself, tech companies did, taking emotionless advantage of you at your lowest and finding ways (inadvertent or otherwise) to *keep* you there. The affordances of social media privilege the worst of the worst, and our norms for platform use only facilitate them.

***

Except perhaps even this idea is a little too neat. "The Algorithm," complete with the definite article giving it the air of some otherwise unnameable Elder God, is blamed for all online social ills. There's good reason for this, of course, but we remain social and *socialized* creatures. After so many years of Web 2.0, our habitual usage patterns don't disappear. Even in the absence of algorithms, the choice of who to follow can create a resonating chamber of venting and despair.

Bluesky again offers a case study. Its timeline (or "skyline" as the locals call it) is not algorithmic; it's chronological and based on your follows. Various "feeds" you subscribe to can curate it further, or add algorithmic selection back into the mix, but your basic feed is "Following." And my "Following" feed (in between the humour and shitposting) is full of the same doom-posting, the same desperation, the same people crowd-funding to make rent, the same gut reactions to awful news stories, the same venting and self-care gone horribly awry, and, in short, the same solipsism that one finds on Twitter.

Algorithms might make it worse, but we are fully capable of doing this to ourselves, even without their help.

***

Still. Our hearts and minds remain our own. We *can* defend them against colonization by hate-campaigners, who feed on our despair like a demon in a German fairy tale. Social media is good at surrounding us with shimmering mirages of certainty and ubiquity, as if what we see there is the truest glimpse into the hearts of people everywhere. But it is not. Even on Elon Musk's Twitter, the hordes of bigots are a digital trick of the light, a minority within a minority far removed from the lives and beliefs of ordinary people.

Turning back to transphobia: Trans people (far more than ever in the past) are still building lives for themselves, even amidst the cavalcade of hate; and many people (also far more than ever in the past) are fighting for our right to do so, in courthouses, libraries, coffee shops, and state houses. After all, every time a group defends a drag queen or trans event from right-wing agitators, it's made up of plenty of cis people.

And I do mean *plenty*. The 2022 US elections proved that; Republicans made transphobia a central platform plank, and many of their Extremely Online agitators predicted this would be the secret sauce allowing the GOP to reach whole new voting blocs, leading to a "red wave" at the polls. They then lost winnable gubernatorial races across the country, barely captured the House, experienced shocking flips in previously safe Congressional territory, and couldn't even gain control of the Senate. It was one of the best midterm performances for the party in the White House in decades — even more astonishing when you considered President Biden's anemic popularity and the shaky economy.

The 2023 elections then doubled down on those results. Kentucky governor Andy Beshear won a deeply red state by a comfortable margin against a Republican who made transphobia a core theme. Ohioans voted to enshrine a right to abortion in their state constitution in the face of claims it'd legalize child "sex-changes" and "mutilation."

MAGA is Extremely Online, but most of the public isn't. Social media is real, but it is *not* a microcosm of the world. The timeline can make you believe that the unbelievably weird people ranting about baby sex-changes represent some vast army of voters. But such a distorted perspective leads to little more than one thing: panic.

***

"Panic is rarely a good organizing or communication strategy," ACLU communications strategist Gillian Branstetter told me. "I think there's a sense amongst some trans folks online that if they ring the bell loud enough, then people will come to help. And that can, combined with just the incentives that are built into a lot of these social media platforms, elevate the most alarmist takes and voices, however ungrounded in reality they might be."

In our wide-ranging conversation, Branstetter (who is herself on the front lines of combatting the transphobic legislative onslaught and describes it as a full-time job "staring into the abyss") nevertheless urged a gentle reminder that what one sees online isn't a complete picture.

"I do wonder," Branstetter suggested to me, "if people are losing sight of the frame and getting lost in the picture." The frame being social media's conflict-driven emphasis on bad news. She added that people — especially trans people — were at risk of "not seeing the ways they're being guided towards certain ends [by Twitter]."

And there it is: that nameless, *unreasoning* terror that paralyzes us as a community. "Ask yourself if social media has an incentive to connect you with other people," Branstetter told me, "or if their incentive is to isolate you and to disconnect you from the people nearest to you and best equipped to support you." A cacophony of voices singing one note of despair can leave you feeling more alone than if you were never online at all.

However, Branstetter pointed to an alternative. "Trans joy," she told me, "is most necessary when it feels most impossible. I've spoken to the families who've been targeted by [government] agencies. I have listened to parents beg for their children's lives in federal court. I stare into the abyss of the current political situation every single day. I am not ignorant to what we face. But that's only made it more urgent that we are being clear and holistic in our practice."

As she suggests, one thing that might help is some vision on these platforms of lives well-lived, of what trans thriving looks like, and of what we're fighting for. Amplifying our joy is amplifying our humanity; it is an antidote to terror, if not a viral one.

This is especially useful, as Branstetter also pointed out to me, for those trans people who rely on social media to have any sense of community at all. It's important for those who live in relative isolation, in rural counties or conservative areas. Even more intensely, it's important for trans young people. As sociologist Tey Meadow put it over a decade ago, we need "inspiration for the kids who are still here . . . they need stories of teenagers just like them who are safe and happy *now*."

Insofar as this sort of positivity is a desirable goal, every trans person who's ever posted a cute selfie is doing their part. As is anyone who's posted their weddings, graduations, parties, new homes, families, smiles, or the beauty that transition made possible.

Let's be careful, though. I don't want to be a grinch, but posting cute selfies or saying uplifting things about your life is not a substitute for activism. If one thinks that way, it leads to things like the It Gets Better campaign, the decade-old Dan Savage-led social media campaign to tell queer youth that, well, however depressed they're feeling now, it gets better.

Whilst positivity-posting might be preferable to doomposting, it still fundamentally attempts to work through individualist logics, the very kind of ethical pointillism that is so ineffective in these spaces. It's not *really* a solution; it's the paper straw of social media reform. (It also presents a wide target. Whatever good intentions Savage's campaign might have has were swallowed up by

Discourse. What if it *didn't* get better? Why are you ignoring Black trans women and trans sex workers with this rhetoric? It didn't get better for those of us who committed suicide, did it? And quickly enough, we're back in the oubliette.) Positivity posting is, at best, a tweak to personal behaviour that might have a salubrious benefit for someone else. While I still agree with Meadows that we need more individual trans joy on social media— Bluesky does a terrific job with this, weirdly— we also have to remember the difference between individual and collective benefits.

***

Collective joy, the joy that comes from simply being who you are in a community, is harder to come by and harder to portray adequately on social media. Photos of protests or communal events come close, but even then it's difficult to decontextualize them from the individual who posted them. We need to see more trans joy, but we also have to find a greater percentage of it off of open social media platforms, cultivating it in person and in smaller, closed online communities.

These days, whenever I see something terrifying online, I think instead of my storyteller fiancée proposing to me by telling a tale she'd saved for years until she finally offered me her great-aunt's heirloom engagement ring. I think of my friends and girlfriends with their dorky jokes, witty barbs, and unforgivable puns during D&D, and of our embraces after shared moments of triumph. I think of the people who gave me karaoke for my birthday, or zipping up dresses in conference hotels, cocktails after midnight, or the trans girl-friend who's a noir detective disguised as a punk and calls me "doll."

That parliament of memory isn't something that fits easily on social media. This is true even though, in one sense, social media is nothing *but* memory. You might think of weddings, parties, graduations, concerts, all photographed and documented online, and posit: Isn't that enough? The reason it isn't is that we experience our memories as communal; to be at a concert or a party is to be, to some extent, lost in a crowd. Happily so, most times. We draw energy from those around us, if we're having (or collectively remembering) a good time. There's more connection, more instant feedback, more energy to draw from. Thus the fuller, deeper truth of our memories is always tricky to communicate online. A photo alone on social media can't convey that; indeed, it can also induce FOMO in the people watching.

Yes, there is a need to crowd out the doom where and when we can with more uplifting treatments of trans life. Doing so is earnest, it is "good and pure." It is also excruciatingly difficult to make positivity go viral on these platforms with the norms and affordances they've cultivated. It's worth trying, however; not because this uplift is itself political, but because in aggregate it may make real politics more *possible*.

Log Off

***

It's not just joy that aids us, however. It's resistance too.

Trans death can become a spectacle on social media, as it was with legacy media before it. There are too many examples to draw upon, but let's consider the relatively recent suicide of Eden Knight — a vibrant, much-beloved twenty-three-year-old trans woman who used to live in the DC area. She said in her suicide note that her father, a powerful Saudi government official, had hired an independent American intelligence firm to track her down and compel her to detransition before returning her to Saudi Arabia.

Her death has sparked grief across the trans internet, but it also spurred action to get her extraordinary story noticed by the mainstream press. As journalist Katelyn Burns asseverated, however, more is needed than leering over the body of another dead trans woman. "What's really needed is action," she writes. Knight wanted to become a leader in the trans rights movement; she grieved the loss of that dream before she died. If the memory of her life's beauty and joy (before her forced) detransition inspires us to defend ourselves with greater vigour, Knight's dream needn't die with her.

"Mourn the dead; fight like hell for the living" is a venerable slogan used in many minority communities faced with violence. But we don't valorize those who *do* fight like hell for the living nearly enough, with platforms disincentivizing images that may inspire and uplift in favour of those that spark endless debates and threats. It was a young trans hacktivist who published a massive trove of emails showing the collusion of far-right activists and legislators in enacting the recent wave of anti-trans laws. She's only twenty-three and she helped to embarrass some of the most powerful legislators and right-wing agitators in the country. If she can do it, so can you.

Or consider Australia, where the public turned out in spectacular fashion to protest a speaking tour by a far-right transphobe, Kellie-Jay Keen. In Hobart, the capital of Tasmania, she met such a vigorous and colourful protest representing the gamut of the state's civil society that even the Rupert Murdoch-owned Tasmanian *Mercury* covered it sympathetically, with a front page of cheerful, trans flag-waving protesters over the headline GENDER DEFENDERS.

These are ideas that inspire, a reminder that there is joy in resistance. *This* is what one does in the face of reckless hate.

***

When I say this, it may sound as though I'm arguing that you should engage with social media *more*, not less. So what does "logging off" mean in this context? It means embedding yourself in your *own* context as much as possible.

Both of the examples I've given — of the terror experienced by trans people, and of the terror experienced by people who fear COVID — are "legitimate" sources of fear. Much like the Great Depression was. Fear is a natural response to the fearful. So often we're told that our fears are irrational, and some arguments (even a few that, superficially, sound like those I've made here — such as the canard that anyone taking COVID precautions is "living in fear" or some such) are constructed to suggest that there is nothing to fear at all. My argument here is not that you should *deny* these gorgons of fear, but that you need to confront with them with tools that are worthy of you. Social media is, by and large, not one of them. Instead, social media specializes in "nameless, unreasoning, unjustified terror which paralyzes needed efforts to convert retreat into advance."

Mid-pandemic panic drove otherwise smart individuals to distraction against a threat that is, for now, irradicable. On a political level, the panic sapped ferment for lasting change. Terror produces mass panic, but it is also profoundly individual, and social media excels at the individualistic. Fear of a threat is easy to instill; it's far harder to organize a collective response against it. Social media crowdsources millions of scary stories and frightens millions more into thinking they're next. And these platforms really give you one, and only one, tool with which to exercise a false sense of control: yelling.

Cholera was not defeated by individual shaming, but by structural improvements to towns and cities. Infrastructure saved us. It ensured clean water became an expectation, not a personal responsibility. The parallel for COVID-19 is improving ventilation and air purification. But instead of something like a Green New Deal to begin the slow, boring work of improving ventilation in buildings, we got endless hectoring about how "we're STILL IN A PANDEMIC."

Just as we don't expect a random convention-goer dressed as Princess Peach to be responsible for their own clean drinking water or toilet facilities, we should not expect them to purify their own air. It's a fundamentally impossible task. I suspect a lot of people on social media might well agree with this, but then find themselves yet again locked into endless Discourse on "WEARING A FUCKING MASK."

The World Health Organization's constitution begins: "Health is a state of complete physical, mental and social well-being and not merely the absence of disease or infirmity." So much social media discourse has fixated merely on the absence of disease and not on a road map towards that new and better world that *could* arise as a lasting legacy to the tragic loss of so many millions. The implications for the fight against climate change are similarly dire. It's not hard to imagine social media's "contribution" to that fight: more individualistic shaming and therapeutic doomsaying at the expense of collective action.

Meanwhile, addressing the onslaught against the trans community is going to require more than obsessive doomsaying, especially the kind purveyed by a handful of trans writers who specialize in the We've Already Lost beat. Headlines like IT'S GOING TO TAKE SEVERAL MIRACLES TO STOP THE REPUBLICAN PARTY FROM TURNING AMERICA INTO HUNGARY or THE END OF TRANS AMERICA COMES INTO FOCUS tell a story all their own, and it's not one where citizens have any agency. *That* does transphobes' work for them, building up their legend, defeating us before we've even had a chance to fight back.

If you're afraid, you need to volunteer in your communities — and to use social media *only* to facilitate narrow goals of mutual aid, to find people in need of help and give it to them. We're going to need people with cars, spare couches, disposable income, and hands they're willing to get dirty. Not with blood, but with grease, sweat, and tears.

Why not blood? Well, that's what the next chapter is about.

Up Against the Wall

The "oubliette of terror" that I described in the previous chapter is a kind of torturous, psychic alchemy, converting every conceivable emotion into leaden fear. This slow torment can lead you down a number of roads you didn't think your mind was capable of paving. One of the bleaker roads — the kind with the flickering lanterns that would qualify as "heavy-handed symbolism" in a horror movie — is the one that leads you to a backwoods shed full of AR-15s.

We are living in unquestionably dramatic times, and when you keep hearing it's the end of the world, well . . . there's plenty of empirical evidence to support the claim. Just take a peek out the window during fire season — something you likely *have* now as a recurring feature of your life when you didn't just a few years ago. How could one *not* think we're living at the end of the world?

And of course we all know what happens during apocalypses, don't we? So it can seem reasonable to think, all of a sudden, that you should go to a gun range and practise some self-reliance in anticipation of the coming zombie apocalypse/ water wars/Ragnarök fight against resurgent fascism.

Or perhaps you're a more sober thinker. There's still the possibility of the kind of apocalypse humanity has faced for centuries: the ends of civilizations, the bleak dawns of tyrannical empires and despotisms. The way the world ended in 1933 in Germany, 1939 in Spain, the late '60s in China, or perhaps 1973 in Chile or Myanmar in 2021: the worst of the worst ascend to power and proceed to *use it*, with violence and vengeance. If you're reading this book, you would likely have been near the top of the endless "lists of enemies" used by such regimes. An intellectual, a member of a despised minority, a would-be dissident.

If such a disaster comes to pass (and it can feel as if we're lurching towards that again, can't it?), words will fail us catastrophically. So will the law; it'll belong to *them*. The fascists will have deadly power and seem to know how to use it; they've done it before and will do so again. You're bombarded with images of right-wing militias, the most extreme bigots, the ugliest thoughts from the ids of people you never would've thought much of in the first place. You see violence, you see hatred, you see *promises* of even greater violence, and then every so often you see some terrorist attack or mass shooting committed by someone who, inevitably, has a terrible social media history littered with rants against whichever minority the right-wing media decided to hate that week.

In such circumstances, it can be hard not to look admiringly at the one thing that has always seemed to stop fascists dead in their tracks. Literally. Armed resistance. So why not get a little bit of that power for yourself? To protect yourself, and your family, from evil people who wish you harm? Isn't the Second Amendment there for *you* too — and isn't that what it's for? Arming the citizenry against tyranny?

In the US, in this exact moment of pitched terror about the resurgence of fascism and the impending climate apocalypse, there is a very real belief among a bunch of frightened queer people and leftists that all the extremists who cheered on the execution of trans people, or the rape of a celebrity, who called a white nationalist terrorist a martyr for the cause, will come after *them*, and that resistance will only come from the barrel of a gun. In reality, they're simply soothing themselves with another private non-solution to a collective problem, sold to them by social media with all the ruthless precision of a targeted ad.

I can rehearse the litany of anti-gun arguments here at nauseating length. I can point out that, in the context of the United States as it exists today, the kinds of guns you can easily access are, at best, recreational, hobbyist toys, and that at worst they can harm you and your loved ones, or be used to kill innocents. I can tell you that a deadly weapon in the house is statistically more likely to be deadly to its owner or to the people they're trying to protect: small children who don't know any better;

suicidal loved ones who might find an easy way out in your bedside drawer; or you yourself when you don't fully appreciate why your gun has a safety. I can point out that a gun in your hand makes you a different kind of person. Someone with a gun, in a dangerous situation, may see only targets. I can even deliberately leave some made-up esoteric fact in that list of arguments, about a hidden trigger, or a proximity-mine chamber, or the steel-tipped dilithium crystal in a specific assault pistol, just to make a gun nut's day, because they'll be able to point out that I got some detail of their favourite weapon wrong.

To engage in such a discussion, however, is to get into exactly the kind of endlessly repeating online argument about guns that I instead want to analyze. What I want to ask is a second-order question: How did social media get us here?

***

American gun-nuttery can feel singular, but its social media manifestation, particularly among marginalized people, is of a piece with the other phenomena discussed in this book. However, it's worth dwelling on the uniquely American form of this wider tendency because — unlike the guillotine of so many Extremely Online leftist fantasies — a gun is easily acquired in the US.

If you live in Canada, Australia, New Zealand, or Europe (including the UK, despite its best efforts) it'll be worth your time to be empathetic here, rather than using the material that follows to act all smug about how superior your country's so-called way of life is. The particular American logic of gun ownership I'm about to describe also keys into certain individualistic, violent longings that are common to *many* cultures, including your own. There is a darkness here that laces through many of the loudly expressed fantasies of violence that propagate on social media, expressed by people all over the world.

Nevertheless, there are a few things that must be said about the particular role that guns play in the psyche of Americans. First, the frontiersman fiction about guns in this country, the idea that they defend your "homestead" against marauding "invaders," is a vision inextricably linked with the history of genocide against Indigenous people. There is no escaping this simple fact. There is no homestead myth without ethnic cleansing, no "cowboys and Indians" games without Native Americans and First Nations people to play the foil, and no frontier to "defend" without Native peoples to defend it *from*. Similarly, the idea of presumably white homeowners defending "their property" is inextricably linked to an imaginary of Black and brown criminals; witness every fantasy about self-defence expressed in right-wing media and you'll find plenty of examples of the genre.

This particular pair of narratives is what founds contemporary understandings of the American Second Amendment. In sum: guns are for killing "marauding" brown people. Every fiction spewed by 2A advocates in the US flows from this point. When they say the Second Amendment protects the First, they mean their right to kill non-white people with impunity guards their right to say anything they please without so much as the tiniest social sanction. Any statements they make about guarding against "tyranny" should be understood in the same light: the loudest advocates, in truth, are demanding their right to shoot any elected officials or civil servants who have the temerity to be non-white and/or advance equality and justice in the US.

Second, the secret sauce of American gun-nuttery is that its — largely white, rural, conservative — exponents are wholly backed up by the very state that their "Second Amendment protects the First" ideology is supposed to oppose. They triumph, not because of their innate political acumen or even their marksmanship, but because the cops either look the other way or actively aid them whenever they go marauding with all their haphazard, half-drunk revenge fantasies.

If you believe in any ideal or value even slightly to the left of the SS, you will not be afforded the same protections. That alone makes your job as a law-abiding leftist gun owner infinitely harder. Your gun will simply not be *allowed* to be used politically in the way that, say, Kyle Rittenhouse's was. In an age where the state wields tanks, armoured vehicles, heavy armour, drones, helicopters, aural weapons, radar, and every firearm under the sun, this state of affairs is untenable when measured against your solitary rifle. That's true for all the far-right 2A wankers too, of course, except that, as I said, they're in on the con. They're not *actually* fighting the state. They're fighting the state's enemies and calling *them* tyranny; they're abetting genocide, police brutality, and the enforcement of capital. That's why they're allowed to get away with so much. In theory, the Second Amendment should protect all Americans' right to own guns equally, but it doesn't. Non-white people, leftists of all backgrounds, and anyone else who doesn't fit the aforementioned frontiersman narratives have all taken up arms only to be literally cut down by the state, without a single peep from the NRA in defence of people who ought to be, by all rights, their fallen martyrs.

***

The people I'm about to scold here (and indeed anyone who's paid more than a nanosecond's attention to current affairs at any time in the last century or two) *should* understand this. And yet, somehow, they have been convinced they are the exceptions to this way of thinking. They think the Second Amendment will *also* help them, that it will include and protect them too. There's an obvious lie baked into this self-soothing promise: the idea that the gun will do for you what it does for the angry, far-right "patriots," that you'll be allowed to use it in the same ways as them, to get one over on them. Or at least to force a stalemate.

Social media is what's selling that particular lie, of course. It can feel more authentic because the filters are not as obvious as they are on, say, the nightly news, whose narrow lenses we might more easily identify — the way they may overemphasize local crime or the moral panic *du jour*. Social media, on the other hand, gives an unassailable illusion of authenticity. It can feel as though it's offering a privileged glimpse into the minds of people you wouldn't ordinarily meet.

It can feel like the collective canary in the coal mine of society.*

I know how profoundly unsettled I was when some washed-up former MMA fighter called for executing anyone who aided in gender-affirming care and a bunch of Elon Musk Era bluecheck accounts replied with enthusiastic affirmations. But this was not a genuine poll of the population, and once again the terroristic effect of seeing 20 tweets in sequence overrode one's inherent understanding that 20 is, in fact, a smaller number than 330,000,000.

Social media surrounds you with the terror of an impossible fight against this magnified vision of resurgent fascism, while pitching one individualistic non-solution after another. In some cases it pitches the hope that you can get a leg up on

....

* It doesn't help that sometimes the canary really was trying to tell us something. GamerGate, for instance, appeared to portend the pandemic of neo-fascism all over the world — from the US to India to Russia to the Philippines. But, as with Nate Silver, one solid prediction does not an oracle make.

the coming horrors by buying a gun, ammunition, and a spot at your local gun club. What you'll actually get is a false sense of security, and all the attendant risks of private gun ownership that will put you and everyone in range in mortal danger.

This, ultimately, is one consequence of spending time in the oubliette of terror. Even if you're the most dependent of social media addicts, you have to re-enter the world *at some point*, but the ceaseless torture sessions will have left their mark on you. They'll leave you contemplating certain things you never would've before. You don't want to bring an allegation of "microaggressions" to a gunfight, do you, after all?

In a perverse way, this discourse is the ultimate proof of the futility of social media wankery. You can't "call out" a terrorist, or shame someone out of mass murder, or dogpile a war criminal. Some part of you recognizes that something more vital is required, some greater force that can meet theirs. But instead of collective organization, instead of *politics*, social media expertly sells you one more individual solution, one more thing you can buy that offers a sense of tactile control — just like masks for the pandemic, or the right *eldritch* language for solving [insert *-ism* here], or calling out an individual bad guy to achieve a similar goal. A thousand points of light in the infinite dark.

A gun is the apotheosis of this search for a universal solvent. The symbol of ultimate political power, encapsulated into a device that fits in your hand. The judge, jury, and executioner's power of presidents, prime ministers, ancient cult leaders, and emperors, all for the low, low price of US$150 per month, with 0% APR. With one individual choice and one individual hit to your credit report, you can fashion a bulwark against the gathering dark. And suddenly, if you think about it, the lunacy of your conservative relatives buying gold and guns makes perverse sense. By that time, if you're lucky, you'll realize you're on the wrong side of the looking glass.

***

Even as we gorge ourselves on deadly serious topics and grieve and panic about them, many of us — especially in marginalized communities on open social media — find ourselves tempted towards unserious responses. If the world seems like a dark joke at our expense, what kind of cuck do you have to be to take it too seriously? You'll only speak like your oppressor, without the benefit of being paid for it. So, you ironize, you mock, you degrade, you piss. Online memeification bleeds everything dry of the uncool seriousness that is anathema to virality.

The problem is that this mentality infects even what you *try* to take seriously. Like guns. On open social media it's easy to give in to simplistic narratives of glory and triumph through transformative violence. When that is combined with the online posture of being too cool to care, soaking oneself in irony like a Molotov rag, violence turns into something less than real. Even when an act of violence is completely justified — like the on-camera rearranging of Richard Spencer's face — it only *becomes* so famous because it's a tightly packed explosive of symbolism, readily intelligible, easily replayed, and able to gain high velocity online. Add in some out-of-context Frantz Fanon quotes and you're golden. The short, sharp cracks of violence are perfect memes, as aerodynamic as bullets, and just as unsubtle. Unmistakable. A literal punchline.

Add to that a heap of political news and a whole lot of doomscrolling and you get a perfect recipe for becoming the kind of person who *definitely* shouldn't own a gun. It's easy to posture online, easy to joke about who belongs "up against the wall," easy to fume about who should die and post about it for clout. It's infinitely harder to stand there, faced with a real human being, and pull the trigger.

Imagine for a second actually trying to use that gun on an actual person. Ask yourself what in your life, truly, has prepared you for that kind of decision. What in your life has prepared you for the consequences if you get it wrong? What has prepared you to take a shot in a chaotic crowd? What has prepared you to feel, in your bones, that you're hitting the right person? And, finally, what has prepared you to come back and remain the kind of person who can live in a just world? Even if that just world is your own little island of paradise with your loved ones or your family, chosen or otherwise. Will you ever be the person they love, again? Or will you always go back, tirelessly, to that moment where you pulled the trigger and ended another human being's life? And all this is assuming that you, yourself, survive, and aren't thrown in prison to be traumatized further.

None of that would make for a good social media post. It wouldn't go viral, and it certainly wouldn't make anyone laugh. There are, of course, ways to glean gallows humour from your PTSD. But if you try to do that, then it starts you right back on the path of exsanguinating the seriousness from a fundamentally serious issue. When it's a joke, it becomes safe. Easier to commodify, more propulsive. It loses the capacity to shock, to arouse one's moral sensibilities. And round and round we go.

* * *

This is why Bluesky's numerous moderation controversies have frequently involved questions of "ironic" violence. There's the "beat you to death with hammers" post, discussed previously, and then a particularly infamous one where a user was banned for telling the moderator staff to 'turn around and face the wall," accompanied by a photo of Ernest P. Worrell from the *Ernest* films holding a gun. That user is still treated (ironically, of course) as a departed saint of shitposting, and "Ernest-posting" — posting that image or using the words "face the wall," just at a new, ironic remove — is a common meme on the platform as of this writing.* And then there's the recent drama over a different user posting, again to the site's moderators, that she hoped they were shot and fed to dogs. Ironically, of course. It's not *real*, it's just posting! She was banned too. She then became the next martyred saint, until her return a few days later — cue a raft of memes about her being the Messiah.

In its way, all the posting was terribly funny. It's hard to avoid snickering at moderators who seem so terminally uncool that they can't discern the difference between posting and a genuine death threat. And anyway, intemperate and careless speech about murder long predates the internet. How many times have you heard, or even said, "Oh, I could *kill* him," about someone who was merely annoying?

But the process by which we become inured or desensitized to the reality of violence is accelerated dramatically on social media. No, it's nothing new; there was worry about television doing exactly this, or computer games. But social media's overtly discursive aspects provide a unique window into the compounding of that desensitization. How many times will you get to see violence used as a joke online, and how long will it be until it

....

* When Bluesky opened up, he returned, like a figure of posting legend. By all appearances, he's on good behaviour—and quite nice, at that. It's a reminder that one indiscretion is hardly definitional of one's life; but it does underscore that it's as strange to *valorize* the indiscretion as it is to completely condemn a person for it.

becomes a joke to *you*? As with so much else, the numbers are bigger and the timelines more compressed.

What makes social media different from previous iterations of mass media is how immersive it is — and, unlike video games, it has unbeatable verisimilitude. It *is* your real life; it *is* your world. You get involved. You're in it, and it's in you (with apologies to all the hornyposters; you can have that one for free). Furthermore, unlike past violent media, it has the ability to promote ideas down to very pointillist levels. You no longer need to agonizingly translate, say, *Rambo* into a leftist fantasy of your own. Now it's simply *supplied* to you directly, with no filter or mediation.

There are movies, art installations, and video games that explore the idea of complicity, turning your own desires, movement, and inputs against you as you experience the work, forcing you to confront yourself. But social media doesn't just do this constantly; complicity is *all it is* most days. It's as participatory and immersive as it gets. Irony becomes a coping mechanism in this context, a way of insulating yourself from the phantasmagoria you've inserted yourself into, a way to cope with the doomscroll of apocalyptic events — and, in the end, a way to distance yourself from your own humanity.

In so doing, you'll be induced to post in ways that help others do the same. Because your humanity and theirs is what's making you all feel so terrible when you look at images of children under rubble in Gaza, say, or hear a story about someone struggling with long COVID, or the next time you read a social media post announcing the suicide of another queer person, or the story of a woman gang-raped on an Israeli kibbutz, or the enormity of millions of dead amidst a pandemic, or thousands dead in a climate-change-induced natural disaster...on and on and on. You cope with rageposting, with denial, and with irony. In time, even something like Hamas can become a meme, or you can be led towards simple revolutionary fantasies of violence that only ever hurts the "right" people. Social media erodes our sensitivity to violence in the worst ways.

***

It also doesn't teach you *how* to use a gun. I don't just mean marksmanship: arguably the least important of the many skills a responsible gun owner needs. You have to be the kind of person who overcomes her survival instinct to run towards rather than away from a deadly situation; who has a clear enough head to be more help than hindrance when she arrives; who has excellent trigger discipline and can accurately assess the situation even as she's surrounded by chaos and potentially faced with someone who will kill her, and you need to do *all* this in the space of seconds, *while* being able to take down your opponent, *while* avoiding innocent bystanders. Only then, will your marksmanship come into play.

The violent, revolutionary cosplay encouraged by social media teaches you precisely none of this. And it certainly doesn't teach you that there's a certain amount of violence one must do to oneself in order to *become* good at all these things. Overcoming a basic survival instinct and knowing how to pull a trigger safely and effectively require deadening parts of yourself that aren't easy to restore. And yet, if you *don't* do that, a loaded gun in your hands is as much a threat to yourself and the people you're trying to help as it is to any of the Bad Guys.

The people who protect drag-queen story hours may or may not be so rigorously well-trained. But I've known many people on the left whom I *would* trust with a gun — and those people could, in a pinch, save a life under the right conditions. Becoming one of them is potentially a worthwhile endeavour, but it's not memeable, and it's not what's really being encouraged by "ARM [INSERT MINORITY GROUP HERE]" rhetoric. Not for nothing, but such people also tend to keep a low profile on social media.

Indeed, I've started to feel that those memes are the "carbon footprint" of the far left. BP gave us the idea of an individual carbon footprint, all the better for getting you to fret about taking an airplane instead of pressuring them to stop their destruction of the planet. Arms merchants didn't invent "ARM [INSERT MINORITY GROUP HERE]" but they may as well have. They certainly benefit from it. Even as their corporate boards fund the politicians and movements that make everyone from queers, to Jews, to Muslims, to women afraid, they then get to reap the financial rewards of those same communities buying their products in *response* to that very fear.

***

Like so much else in this space, capitalist logics have permeated everything, even notionally radical, anti-capitalist politics. We all have to survive somehow, of course, but that basic truth doesn't absolve us from our obligation to see the strings by which we've been moved, our obligation to recognize when we're being *sold* on something. Especially when the logic of a salesman begins to permeate the ideology that's supposed to *liberate* us from his schemes.

The network effects of social media are not to be underestimated. It's why so many corporations (or "brands") now have snarky, meme-y social media accounts, using your jokes and ironic posturing to convince you that Mitt Romney was right: corporations are people, just like you and me. The effectiveness of this tactic is something we — myself included – tend to underestimate. But the same people who scoff at this try-hard corporate behaviour often fail to recognize the subtler ways in which capitalism weaponizes authenticity. Word-of-mouth advertising was always a holy grail for anyone with a product to sell (by the by, if you're enjoying this book, tell your friends!). Social media ensures that word-of-mouth advertising can spread far and wide if it manages to key into the zeitgeist.

What they're out to do is to sell you on some soothing little luxury you can buy to feel better about yourself. I'm hardly immune — I acquired half my bra collection for this reason. But a bra isn't going to kill me or my fiancée. And I'm not ennobling the frilly little things with political purpose. While we can all fall prey to targeted ads (however sophisticated we fancy ourselves), we are at greater risk when we allow the collective surge of social media Discourse, with its patina of authenticity, to sell us private, personal purchases as solutions to vast social problems.

Guns are no exception. This is why people who would cringe at a misfired Facebook ad, or at the bullshit of the Wendy's Twitter account, or at the unbelievably cloying pantomime of big brands high-fiving each other on Meta's Threads, are nevertheless to be found nodding sagely when some self-styled Marxist-Leninist with a hammer and sickle in their bio starts extolling the virtues of Smith & Wesson.

All the while, those companies depend on your virtuous authenticity to make gun ownership seem decent, respectable, and, above all, emotionally satisfying and desirable. Despite the resolute political conservatism of arms merchants, I'm quite certain they don't give a good goddamn if a pink-haired catgirl communist is buying up their hunting rifles and tacti-cool handguns. Her money spends just as well. And she can be an unwitting influencer for a whole new market segment. Best of all, from the perspective of the arms merchant, the advertising is *free*.

***

Why do I care so damn much about this? It's not because I hate guns — though I'm hardly someone who'd be on Bushmaster's Christmas list — but because when I see this advice being dispensed regularly and aggressively to transgender people, to *my* people, I do get worried. I worry when a community that is already shockingly vulnerable to mental health crises and suicidal ideation is told to buy the easiest tool with which to commit suicide and keep it in their homes. I worry that for every glorious strike against a fascist, we'll lose ten more of us by our own hands. I worry that instead of building resilience against the hourly assault on our collective sanity, the online trans community (which skews young) is being told to get the most violent quick fix imaginable.

A quick Google search of "arm trans women" brings up oodles of (what else?) merchandise and propaganda for that effort. Stickers, patches, buttons abound. There's an "Arm Trans Women and Jews" T-shirt, a song called "Arm Black Trans Women," as well as some sympathetic news stories that frame the effort of arming queer people more broadly as an act of self-defence against rising hate. New Hampshire Public Radio's Todd Bookman interviewed one organizer of a queer-focused gun group who said, "If the world is dangerous, then you have to be dangerous back. And that very much has pushed me into where I am now." Another person at the same range, going by the pseudonym of "Guardian," said, "If you go far enough left, you get your guns back." And then, of course, there's the inevitable right-wing attempt at ginning up moral panics about someone holding an "Arm Trans Kids" sign at a rally.

Over on Bluesky, posts like

> I would sincerely like to see every queer person and leftist armed. As in with guns. Firearms

or an image macro of an AR-15 superimposed over a trans flag with the words

> ARMED MINORITIES ARE HARDER TO ERADICATE

are fairly commonplace.

Posts like these offer up a certain amount of hope — hope that's priced to move, if the gun enthusiast website I used to confirm the gun's model is any guide. That particular model line is described as "mission-specific, ready-to-go fighting guns with a low price point of $599." Hope from a gun shop, just as long as you don't think too deeply about the actual scenarios in which your private gun ownership truly helps the entire community.

It's worth coming back to the idea of "nameless, unreasoning terror" here. Virtually every trans person I know who's talked about guns or mulled getting one is doing so because they're afraid. Some say this explicitly — and can even name very specific fears. They're dealing with cyberstalkers, or the likes of Kiwi Farms obsessives who combine their hyper-fixations with a frothing prejudice that the authorities care too little about. Indeed, someone I regard as a cream puff and an absolute sweetheart happened to rant to me one night about how ridiculously loose American gun laws were — then she went out and bought a handgun the very next day. She'd been planning to for a while, it turned out; she wants to keep her girlfriend safe from people on the internet who'd been threatening to kill her.

If social media is selling guns to trans people as a solution, it's also supplying us with an endless river of The Problem. Whether it's setting you doomscrolling through one apocalypse of hyper-awareness after another, or providing bigots with ready access to your eyeballs, it's an ouroboros of hellish proportions. Stay on social media to make money; get harassed by bigots who make you genuinely fear for your life, and who have ready access to you *because* of social media; use the money you've earned to buy a hand-gun thanks to being surrounded by agitprop telling you that it'll keep you safe *and* liberate your community. Just look at that context-free image of a resistance fighter looking damn fine in leather, holding a rifle. It worked for them, didn't it? You want some of that power. It'll make you harder to eradicate. Then stay on social media, get harassed by bigots who make you genuinely fear for your life. Here's a world of terrors waiting to get you, and here's an individualized solution wrapped in a flag of your choosing, all for only $599.

***

Once again, like some twisted recurrence of the Golden Ratio, we see the essential structure that is so corrosive to genuine organizing on social media in yet another domain. This individuation, the promise of One Weird Trick (preferably a commodity you can buy) to achieve some valorous end, inhibits real activism and makes collective action significantly harder to achieve — especially when social media is your primary activist tool. In this specific instance, the memeification of violence combined with an inability to meaningfully organize, train, and delegate to people ensures that social media is, ultimately, just finding clever ways to sell us the wares of arms merchants and nothing more.

The problem is that the path of *least resistance* it offers is, well, the path of least resistance. It trades meaningful resistance for individual gratification, often in the form of consumption. Whether it's the near-valueless commodities of internet ephemera like memes, or a $600 rifle, you're being sold on something — something individual that can solve all your problems. But that's not, nor is it ever, what real social activism was supposed to be. We will always need to procure tools, and so long as capitalism exists in some form, we'll have to buy them; but such consumption should never become an end in itself. The problem is that a lot of platform tides wash you out to an online marketplace and then draw you back in for more of the same fearmongering, FOMO, anxiety, and doom that will only lead you to go out and buy something *else* to dull the pain.

Far be it from me to dis dulling the pain; I've lost count of the number of vodka shots I've had while writing this book. But this is, again, about criticizing the lullaby our timelines sing to us: the idea that such palliatives are the only thing worth striving for. It's bad enough when it's garden-variety consumer goods; when we start looking to *guns*, we're in dire straits indeed.

***

So, am I asking you to roll over and die for fascist militias or would-be hate-criminals? Of course not. This isn't even an argument against political violence as such — I once wrote a lengthy essay on the ethics of punching Nazis. But I also recall, in the wake of writing it, a friend of mine — a leftist trans woman herself — lamenting to me that too many of the youth she worked with were too eager to get their hands bloody, that there were risks to one's soul in the pursuit of violence. She regretted that I didn't dwell more on that idea in my writing, which she feared might too easily license a kind of glory-seeking.

Well, several years late, let me try to thread that needle.

Just as with FDR's inaugural, we can say that the subject of the "fear" being described is something that was genuinely worth being afraid of. The terrors of our age are myriad. Who could blame any citizen of goodwill for fearing what lies just around the corner? As Roosevelt also said, "only a foolish optimist can deny the dark realities of the moment."

Indeed, this book is being published on the eve of an election where American democracy itself seems to be at stake, barbarically threatened by people who want to roll back a century of progress and obliterate the rights of women and minorities of all sorts.

And these people *are* violent. They either abet murderers or are murderers themselves. Think of January 6, or Kyle Rittenhouse, or the depredations of the Proud Boys and Oath Keepers. Indeed, think of the way that members of armed far-right groups have taken up the mantle of anti-trans panic and menaced libraries or other venues that hosted drag-queen story hours. Whenever I discuss my own scepticism with respect to guns, I'm often reminded that armed leftists show up to intimidate the Proud Boys right back. And I cheer this on.

But a gun, by itself, is not a solution to fascism, and while there are models in the form of the French Resistance or armed Jewish revolts against the Nazis, it's worth recognizing that there were many roles to be played in all these organizations and uprisings. Combat is the most attention-getting, the easiest to valorize, especially in hindsight. Our feeds will readily present us with images of worthy people wielding arms and looking cool, even sexy — from Black Panthers to the French Resistance to Kurdish militia fighters, and many more besides. What is neglected, as those images get Che Guevara'd into implicit ads for arms manufacturers, is the institutions that stood behind all these heroes, the patient work that has to be done behind the scenes, the parallel infrastructures they were trying to build for their people.

For every gunner, there were many teachers, nurses, cooks, translators, therapists, and countless others, performing these roles professionally or on an ad hoc basis to fill the void left by an absent or hostile state. Uplifting an oppressed people takes more than force of arms — even if, sometimes, you can't do *without* them. It's why street medics and legal observers are so incredibly valuable at protests; you need someone whose skills don't lie primarily in combat to help out with all manner of technical work.

Social media convinces us to lard our whims and tastes with overwhelming political importance, and what gets crowded out is real collective activism. That's not trivial; it's *everything*. For even if one wishes to emulate groups like the French Resistance, it's important to recognize that such groups were *organized*. They were not little people hiding in their homes clutching their guns, waiting for some random Nazis to attack them. They got together, they became cells and units, they formed networks, they became an *organization*. Having a gun isn't a precondition of all that; it is but one possible outcome of doing the organizing *well*. I can think of nothing less effective against fascism than scared, isolated people quaking with guns in hand, not talking to each other or making serious efforts to organize and pool their resources.

But the collective solutions are out there. There are local activist groups who could use the time and energy you spend at the range, or who need resources that gun money could be better spent on. And as far as individual solutions go, exercise and self-defence training will work wonders for both your mental health and your ability to fend off overconfident attackers.

***

We can and should valorize specific acts of worthy violence, like the punching of Richard Spencer, and quickly dispense with the usual hand-wringing about such events. But we should also recognize those moments for what they are: desperate rear-guard actions, carried out by people who know what they're doing and who've accepted a specific role as part of a wider struggle. These are not actions that are meant to bring about change, or even momentary salvation. They're situational moments of self-defence when all else has failed. In order to make them less urgent, less necessary, we must do the hard, boring work of changing the world in our own communities.

Violence, it must be recognized, is sometimes necessary, but it's something else to lust for it. Lusting for violence does terrible things to you eventually. Perhaps you can take that on; perhaps you'll need to, for one reason or another. But the odds are that you *don't* need to, and that — if you're truly afraid of these desperate days — there's much more you can do that will rejuvenate your spirit rather than diminish it. Forming connections with real people in your community is always a good first step. There are many ways to mourn the dead and fight like hell for the living. One is simply to *talk* to the living and be in community with them, to be part of a world that's worth it to *them* to live in. You may be able to do this on social media, and perhaps that's where you'll be called. But you'll do it even better in person.

To do so means leaving behind the edgy glorification of violence on open social media, and even some of the fear; perhaps you can even turn that fear into energy that'll help others. I'm not saying you have to become a pacifist, but if you meet any pacifists — and they are out there, in our communities, quietly working towards a more just world — you should talk to them to get a few ideas. *That's* where you should start.

A Vindication of the Rights of e-Girls

or,

Bluesky Is for the Dolls

There's a particularly interesting bit of world-building amidst the atmospheric chill of the 2006 movie *Children of Men*. The protagonist, living in a post-apocalyptic Britain staggering into oblivion after a fertility virus renders the entire planet sterile, visits his cousin — a government minister — to get some vital documents. His cousin oversees the Ark of the Arts, Britain's last hurrah of stealing art from other countries. It purports to be a repository of the world's great art, spirited away from countries that descended into "chaos" because of the virus.

The movie is an excellent meditation on the kind of xenophobic madness we're all too prone to indulging when confronted by disease, but for our purposes the Ark of the Arts is interesting for other reasons.

You see, it's Bluesky.

***

I've been writing this book at a curious moment in the history of social media: the dying days of Twitter as an independent website and the sudden mass migration of users to other, lesser imitators. Indeed, the reason so many examples in this book come from Bluesky is that it's what I was using at the time — and I say that with all deliberate reference to drugs, of course.

Bluesky became a kind of halfway house for Twitter drama; a place where, like the Ark of the Arts, we stole that which should've been left behind and set it up as if it were glorious. Except, unlike Michelangelo's *David*, which at least has some reasonable claim to glory, it was pointless Discourse-for-the-sake-of-Discourse. Like the idea that white trans women constitute some uniquely virulent vector of racism — a notion that was so tenacious only because a disturbing number of people couldn't grasp the fact that this meme had purchase due to the "trans women" part of the equation and not the "white" bit.

Bluesky quickly came to host all manner of absurd Twitter-like drama, some of which I have described in the preceding chapters — bit players from idiotic scenes like the brouhaha over the woman who served her neighbours chili, for instance, or other actors who tried to stoke up a "Posters' Strike"[20] on Bluesky only to be revealed as sex pests, or harassment ringleaders who moved from Twitter to Bluesky only to continue the ceaseless drama they'd built their sad lives around. Bluesky's beta design, so perfectly imitating most of Twitter's affordances, made this inevitable — an everyone-to-everyone platform where there was no way to add friction to conversations, or to close off the scope of Discourse.

Within the walls of Bluesky's garden, it's as Twitter-esque as it gets; there are few brakes. If you said something, you couldn't control what was done with it, who saw it, when, and how they interpreted it. Your joke could easily lead to sonorously pious Discoursing in a matter of minutes; you'd risk old enemies seeing it; you'd risk people appropriating it in bad faith. You couldn't stop any of it — just like Twitter at its worst.*

Thus, any sufficiently viral post — and on Bluesky, "viral" meant anything more than a few dozen or so likes — could lead to the usual spasms of

....

* I do need to give credit where it's due: One of my favourite features of Bluesky is one of the most frustrating — and it's *good* that it's frustrating. If someone quote-skeets you and you block them, then the quoted skeet disappears for *everyone*. No link. No username. It very efficiently cuts off an avenue of dogpiling harassment. It's frustrating, of course, because despite writing a hundred pages of scolding, I remain a slut for drama and dearly want to see what people were mad about for five minutes. I can't deny, however, that it's better for me, and for the site as a whole, that I'm denied that dubious pleasure. These sorts of tweaks can go some ways towards ameliorating very real problems on platforms like this; it is a speed bump. In order to circumvent this feature, people have to go out of their way to create and post screenshots, for instance. A real possibility, but you have to be dedicated: it's far more involved than simply clicking through to the quoted skeet to give that reprobate a piece of your mind. Yet, as I think the examples I've given throughout this book make clear, even these innovations, these speed bumps, can *only* do so much.

context collapse. Indeed, context would collapse on itself endlessly, like falling dominoes. The degree to which this happened on Bluesky, the speed and intensity, was shocking considering its relatively small population, to say nothing of how the site was walled off from the rest of the world by its strict invite-only system.

The one redeeming feature of this environment was that skeets were not considered news the way many tweets still were, and so the abject stupidity of these kerfuffles was not turned into the business of *New York Times* subscribers or Congressional committees. That sole saving grace managed to contain the damage, like Chernobyl's sarcophagus, but it also made it even more pathetic than usual.

So why stick around? As someone who hopped onto Bluesky with eagerness and posted there with zeal, I know I'm something of a hypocrite. My hope here is to, at least, autoethnographically analyze why so many of us are so repeatedly tempted to leap headfirst into social media spaces, and maybe even, after five chapters of relentless critique of social media, identify some things it may actually have to offer.

It's easy to gesture to practical benefits — to our careers, our pocketbooks, and so on — but deep down most of us, I think, know there's something *less* to it. We don't always bring zeal to those things that make money for us. Such things are often desultory obligations. Social media, on the other hand, is *fun*, for some particularly *Saw*-like value of "fun." The attention is fun, and the posts are often exquisitely funny. We are all Ariel from *The Little Mermaid*: we want to go where the people are. Honestly, it's far from the worst motivation.

As with so many other sites of its kind, Bluesky is good at fomenting and preserving pointless drama in the same way that the Ark of the Arts preserved art amidst a time of despair — and it's terrible at fomenting constructive politics. But that doesn't mean it's devoid of merit. In fact, I want to argue, the so-called frivolity of social media is actually the best hope for using it healthily; and the likes of e-girls are almost certainly running rings, in terms of actual effective good they achieve, around everyone claiming to be doing online activism.

***

We've endured one micro moral panic about social media after another. Remember all the risible pearl-clutching about the "TidePod Challenge," for instance? Or, to take a more recurrent expression, about selfies? Like so much media hand-wringing (written by people who either were about to be, or were already, addicted to social media), it all missed the big picture in favour of scapegoating something that the young 'uns were inexplicably into. And yet, in many ways, selfies represent one of our healthiest interactions with social media.

What gets *derided* as trivial is what is actually the best of all this. Silly pictures of our food, horrible vacation selfies, our silly thoughts on the movie we just saw, threads about reconnecting with a beloved childhood toy, or memes about a video game we're currently addicted to — all of that is, in its own way, beautiful. It's *equal* to the affordances of social media. Selfie-posting can crowdsource a boost to one's confidence, for instance. A social media dopamine hit, but an innocent one. After all, who's being hurt?

One of my frustrations is that many self-appointed critics of online life fixate on the wrong kinds of trivia, scapegoating the silly things done by the silliest users of platforms as being Everything Wrong with Society. If anything, the e-girls*, e-boys, hornyposters, foodstagram freaks, and, yes, even the odd influencer who doesn't let it go to their head, are the exact opposite of The Problem. If I stare at anything long enough, I can find a problem with it. I can see where some capillary of bullshit is feeding into the mains. But in ranking these issues, the assorted "problems" associated with this kind of garden-variety posting

....

* The term *e-girl* has a variety of meanings, most of which constellate around a young woman with an emo aesthetic who makes herself very visible on social media, perhaps as an Instagram influencer or a Twitch streamer. While the term has been around for some time, if *Urban Dictionary* is to be believed, it's increasingly being used to describe a type of femme poster on TikTok: "a girl on tiktok that wears an excessive amount of blush, hearts under their eyes, cute hair, watches anime and dresses kinda Lolita," according to an *Urban Dictionary* definition submitted by "'russ is annoying." My preferred definition incorporates these elements but is also more catholic. Per Wikipedia, the term *e-girl* "was first used in the late-2000s as a pejorative against women perceived to be seeking out male attention online," and it's that idea, that of the bogeywoman, the scapegoat, that I wish to focus on.

are not really worth our social concern. It's only when you need an IV drip of dopamine from beefs, harassment, drama, and much else in that genre that things rapidly take a turn for the Lovecraftian (racism and anti-Semitism very much included). But this raises a real question: Is there a better way to use social media? Can't we be free to enjoy the parts that are actually innocent fun?

***

As of this writing, there's been consternation about the NPC (non-playable character) posting trend on TikTok. By the time you read this, it may already be a dead-and-gone bit of cyber ephemera, lost like tears in the rain, et cetera. But, essentially, it's a trend where TikTokkers act like NPCs in video games, moving stiffly, repetitively, and responding to stimuli (and specifically to fan interactions) with pre-recorded "barks". For instance, on a Twitch stream, someone might donate a dollar, which triggers an ice cream cone emoji to appear, and the NPC influencer will go "Yum! Ice cream!" with all the cartoony cadence of a video game character programmed to respond to stimuli in that way.

This repetitiveness was critical. People could post emojis, pay money, or otherwise interact with a streamer to make them "act like an NPC," issuing these repetitive lines or gestures as though they were a character in a relatively unsophisticated video game.

It's all rather silly and weird. I remember joking with a friend who introduced me to the trend that this was the day I ceased to understand what The Kids were up to, despite having played the video games that originated these tropes since I was a literal kid myself. But, in point of fact, it's actually not that hard to understand. It's wacky, it's viral, it's memeable (i.e., a simple format begging for imitation and iteration).

Naturally, because people were having fun, those who were committed to using these platforms as eminently *political* had to swoop in to wag their fingers. One rather self-serious woman, who, without any irony, did her makeup in a state of undress as she lectured TikTok, suggested that this trend risked sexualizing minors who imitated it, because it amounted to prototypical sex work. You see, teenagers might act like NPCs for men who gave them money to act in a robotic way that these men might then get off to. This is, of course, theoretically possible. But if we're policing internet content because some guy might potentially jerk off to it, we'd have to ban the entire web. This is the perfect microcosmic illustration of the *real* problem: a trivial bit of fun makes some people happy and nets them a few bucks (maybe), which is then hoovered up into the purgatory of Discourse to be endlessly debated by people who would rather do *that* instead of actual politics.

I found the NPC trend weird. Sometimes delightfully so, sometimes in a way that had me recoiling from my screen. But, in the end, it was harmless. And it's probably gone by now anyway, consumed whole by some new challenge or viral trend that might fuel a hand-wringing bit of copy in the *National Review* or the *New York Times* or the *New Statesman*. I'd rather we just had a bunch of people going "Yum! Ice cream!" on TikTok than a larger gaggle of people debating the moral harms of that behaviour while pretending it *matters*.

It is absolutely true that people who participate in viral trends, or who hornypost, or who share trivial details about their days and their lives, are doing so in response to the same affordances I criticized earlier. But, crucially, what they give up to such inducements is fundamentally harmless. I post a picture of my amazing sheet-pan chicken with jammy tomatoes to show off a bit because I know sexy pictures of food get the likes. Where's the harm? I'm not making the food *for* social media, I'm making it because my fiancée and I need to eat; the photo's a happy side effect. Of course, once you descend the dark path of influencing, you may start to do everything "for the 'gram," but that does not, in point of fact, describe the vast majority of social media's users.

And what's true of foodposters is true of hornyposters as well. When a person's income depends on their hornyposting, it can get more than a little complicated for sure; how much of this is *you* versus your landlord's insatiable need for three-quarters of your income? I'm not blind to that exigency. Equally, I don't see the inherent social media-based harm here, and economic relationships are rarely completely healthy. If you need to make money, this is a very legitimate way of doing it, and the potential harms are no greater than if you tried to do this sort of work in person (arguably far lesser, due to the lack of physical interaction; others may argue that the endurance of online images can harm long-term career prospects or facilitate harassment and revenge porn). In any case, the harms are not *social*. You're doing this for money, you're not pretending this is politics, not pretending it's an adequate zero-calorie substitute for street activism. You want to be an exhibitionist, and you want to be paid for it. Good for you. Get that bag. *This* sort of posting was never the heart of the problem.

***

In fact, when I think about Bluesky's greatest successes, they all lay in variants of hornyposting and uncategorizable silliness. They used platform affordances to further private aims harmlessly.

The aims of such posting — whether it's me with my chicken, me with my sexy vaccine selfie (no, you can't see it), or my many mutuals with their trivial lifeposting, selfies, and live tweets of video games — are fundamentally individual. Individuality, in itself, is not a sin. The question is whether the individual focus comes at the expense of something more important. In all the aforementioned cases, it absolutely does not. But in the cases of those who transmute real, vital politics into this individualist medium and somehow expect collective results . . . yes, such efforts *do* come at the expense of things that truly matter. The e-girls aren't the problem; people who think The Revolution will come from a critical mass of shitposting and harassment *are*. You can get so deep into that mindset that you start to forget what real politics *is*, even as these platforms allow you to theoretically follow it in minute detail.

Ironically, the kind of person who might be considered the most frivolous may be the most effective when it comes to marrying affordances with goals. Take Dylan Mulvaney, a trans woman influencer who came under the most vicious assault from the far right. She was attacked for no reason other than that she was visibly, ostentatiously happy while being visibly, ostentatiously trans online. She was showing off trans joy, a trans life worth living, a trans life that was defined by giddy, silly happiness rather than rage and sorrow.

For her evident lack of troubles, she was attacked by the far right with especial vitriol. But even some leftist trans people online mocked and excoriated her for being "cringe." What did that mean? Well, she used social media to achieve something that had limited but genuine value: showing a vision of trans life that was *not* defined by tragedy. I wouldn't go so far as to call it activism, but it *was* useful. It was *equal* to social media's capabilities, thus it could do something constructive. The action in question could give more than it took away from us.

Trivial bits of fun are often scapegoated for social decline. The youths are too busy being e-girls instead of changing the world! But that's not a problem; fun is fun, basking in attention is delightful, and we've been doing it since the dawn of time. The problem — the thing that *actually* saps our vitality for changing the world for the better — is pretending that posting is essential to making it happen. It is, ironically, the most self-serious uses of social media that are the most toxic and destructive to serious macropolitical aims.

Frivolity is more apt for social media, it's a better fit for the tool in question. Serious-minded activists depending exclusively or primarily on social media for their work are like surgeons using a pen to stitch a wound, or a writer using a scalpel to edit their proofs. You may be able to find an inventive way to make it happen, against all odds, and with a lot of creativity. But at every step you'll be fighting the fundamental design of the tool in question, in a way you wouldn't if you used a tool that was simply *made* for the job.

***

It's rare that self-referential online activism is anything more than onanism. Think of Occupy Democrats' turgid repetition of "RT to show you disagree with Mitch McConnell!" or similar genres of self-fluffery. One rare instance of self-referential online activism actually working was the Drop Kiwi Farms and End Kiwi Farms campaigns, because their target was an online entity weaponizing the affordances of open platforms to harass their preferred victims. When some of its victims fought back, they won.*

There were two reasons for this: 1) Unlike the vast majority of online activist campaigns, there was a meaningful goal beyond mere engagement. In the case of Drop Kiwi Farms, the goal was simple: get Cloudflare to stop hosting and providing DDOS protection to the site. 2) These campaigns were redirecting the forces Kiwi Farms had weaponized back at them. They crowdsourced pressure on Tier 1 ISPs to de-host these platforms, generating chatter and Discourse that then prompted other Extremely Online entities to act — from journalists who spent too much time on Twitter to tech workers with power to press for change at their firms. It was a rare instance of online activism being genuinely effective.

This illustrates what I am tempted to call Cross's Law of Social Media Activism: you can only use Twitter to solve problems created *on* Twitter. Kiwi Farms generated harassment through open platforms, thus those platforms could be turned around, like a shotgun in a Looney Tunes cartoon, to blast their wielders full in the face. This is not true of most activism, however. Thus, self-referential

....

* Kiwi Farms is a forum devoted entirely to harassing people who they deemed "weird" or "cringe," with a disproportionate focus on transgender women, furries, otherkin, plural people, and the disabled. It's still online, but has been dehosted by so many providers that it limps along in the scuzziest corners of the internet.

online activism should be avoided unless it meets these two key requirements: a clear, achievable goal plus a clear link between the affordances of open platforms and that desired outcome.

And the rest of the time? We should be avoiding any dependency on open social media for serious matters. At the very least, we should never mistake self-promotion for the furtherance of a Cause. Your hyper-visibility is almost certainly not a collective benefit for any marginalized community you are a part of. You being a microcelebrity is *probably* not activism in itself. Your exposure is, at best, tradeable for a little bit of currency that you'll almost certainly need to keep for yourself. Energy spent on these platforms is better devoted to genuine organizing, mutual aid, and more.

***

Meanwhile, the very term *mutual aid* is being colonized in real time by platform Discourse, turned into a synonym for online charity — people pleading for help with their rent or crowdfunding for medical services or unexpected bills. Worthy causes all; donate when you can. It's some small token of solidarity amidst the decaying monuments of capitalism. But it's not "*mutual* aid" in the original sense of the term, which connoted collective action that provided a sustainable, consistent alternative to missing state institutions. Something akin to the way the Black Panthers provided free breakfasts for children through the People's

Free Food Program. Under this new, refined, social-media-ready definition, donating to the Salvation Army could be said to be mutual aid; the Bill and Melinda Gates Foundation could call their next lavishly funded program mutual aid, and... Well, that makes a stronger case against this instance of definition creep than anything else I could write.

But such debauching of needful radical language is a microcosm of what social media does (just think of what happened to words like *triggered* and *gaslighting*). Out of the most urgent necessity, concepts we desperately need to describe broader, collective activism that could really change things are forcibly mutated into individualist forms, edited into genetic material that can truly go viral. Until all that's left is the image, the symbol.

When everything is reduced to imagery and symbolism — and social media *is* a medium of images, even on platforms that feel predominantly text-based — it is easy for politics to be reduced to the gestural. "Platforms are political" is almost axiomatic among online activists and internet scholars alike. But in popular discourse, this frequently gets misrepresented to mean "platforms are political *tools*," implying that they are fully under the control of the user. But even the meanest tool, like a hammer, shapes the way we see the world — hence the very old aphorism you probably just thought of when I mentioned hammers. We neglect the ways platforms use *us*, and the way their political nature is often about channelling our *human* nature towards the needs of capital.

Web 2.0 social media — open platforms that are also walled gardens — seek to proliferate imagery and symbols, all while keeping you wedded to the platform itself. To that end, political uses of platforms get bent into shape by the affordances meant to facilitate that, like quote-tweeting a dunk, or asking people to like and share your content, or contributing to a callout thread with an especially witty reply. Here, visibility is a function of attention. We adopt the idioms of our chosen platforms, both to be understood and to fit in. In that sense, platforms are no different from any number of social spaces. We reconcile ourselves to the group, observe the norms, and, hopefully, become the kind of person who makes meaningful connections therein.

But in face-to-face spaces, that dynamic does not preclude meaningful activism. Online, it keeps us stuck on the platform, seeking it out as the solution to every problem. In turn, that shapes our approach to the world. We need catharsis, so catharsis becomes activism; we want to shitpost, so shitposting becomes activism; we want to clown on someone, so dunks become activism. It's simple enough to ignore that these are all things social media makes trivially easy.

This does not happen out of malice. People are genuinely in need; their grief is genuine; their hopelessness is genuine. They are not scammers, nor are they chasing clout. But they shoehorn needful ideas into the precise shape that benefits them most because that is what a platform built under capitalist conditions has required them to do. And it will do the same to any concept that feels emancipatory — until it finds a way to make scraping by within this system feel progressive, even radical.

All the while, we create value for the companies, but little else.

***

But if this is the case, another question arises. You've surely been hearing, for years, about how social media has accelerated and amplified hate speech, far-right extremism, and so much worse besides. Misinformation, disinformation, and worse — Facebook played a significant role in the Rohingya genocide in Burma, for instance, and Twitter and Facebook are crucial propaganda tools for Hindu nationalists in India. So many seem to agree that social media has made the world worse. And yet I've appeared to argue that social media actually *blunts* our ability to change the world.

Can social media be bad for leftists but good for fascists? How do I square this circle? The answer has to do with the difference between individual and collective change — the very axis my criticism has cut across.

The far right, while having gargantuan collective ambitions, also comprises a scatterplot of individualist desires. They want to hurt people. They want to destroy individuals for the crime of being who they are. They want to obliterate queers, trannies, whores, and more. They count every dead, suicided, or murdered member of some group they hate as a legitimate victory. Directing a mass of angry people at a hapless individual is something that open social media is exquisitely good at, and a neat fit with these goals.

Reactionary movements have always been good at visiting terror on the solitary targets of their hatred, and Web 2.0 has only served to make this infinitely easier. When you think about what online harassment can do — the way it can focus people with the remorseless precision of a spear point onto one hapless body — it's obvious that social media is profoundly useful to those who would want to hurt someone.

Social media allows online fascists to latch on to some "weird" or "degenerate" target, pile-drive harassment into every corner of their life, and force them to flee social media. Once that is achieved, the target only experiences much worse, as the bastards keep intruding on their life: cyberstalking, doxing, swatting, death threats, rape threats, bomb threats — harassment that drives people to distraction, madness, self-harm, despair, and even suicide. And as the fascists do this, they can also go viral, their actions shared by both their supporters and, counter-intuitively, their opponents. Social media's harsh glare magnifies them, making these small people appear positively gargantuan when their shadows dance on the walls of their victims' fantasies.

The far right's overarching goals of Gilead or the Fourth Reich are harder to achieve through social media alone, but their narrow goals of causing extreme pain to their targets? That, it *can* do.

This reactionary blood lust is a global problem. Erin Kissane, a tech journalist and co-founder of the *Atlantic*'s COVID Tracking Project, recently wrote up a history of Facebook's role in fomenting the Rohingya genocide in Myanmar.[21] It's worth reading in full. She cites the words of Mohamad Ayas, a Rohingya schoolteacher and refugee interviewed by Amnesty International. He said, in part:

> We used to live together peacefully alongside the other ethnic groups in Myanmar. Their intentions were good to the Rohingya, but the government was against us. The public used to follow their religious leaders, so when the religious leaders and government started spreading hate speech on Facebook, the minds of the people changed.

Kissane further cites an Al Jazeera documentary on these ethnic tensions by journalist Aela Callan, who in turn interviewed analyst Richard Horsey. Horsey affirmed a key point that I've long tried to make about social media, arguing that tensions between Buddhists and Muslims in the country were very old indeed but that social media ensured "information is readily available and transmissible," and that "every time there's a spark, it's much more likely to turn into a fire."

As you might expect, Kissane's criticism of Facebook is deservedly withering. She writes:

> [Facebook had] been shown example after example of dehumanizing posts and comments calling for mass murder, even explicitly calling for genocide. And [Myanmar-based technologist] David Madden had told Meta staff to their faces that Facebook *might well play the role in Myanmar that radio played in Rwanda.* Nothing was subtle. [emphasis in original]

Faine Greenwood, a journalist and technologist with extensive experience reporting in Myanmar, wrote their own history of Facebook's role in the genocide, and recalled a conversation they had with a taxi driver in 2013:

> [He] asked me what I was in town for, and I told him that I'd come to write about the Internet. "Oh, yes, I've got a Facebook account now," he said, with great enthusiasm. "It is very interesting. Learning a lot. I didn't know about all the bad things the Bengalis had been doing."
> "Bad things?" I asked, though I knew what he was going to say next.
> "Killing Buddhists, stealing their land. There's pictures on Facebook. Everyone knows they're terrorists," he replied.
> "Oh, fuck," I thought.[22]

For some, this will be a familiar story, with echoes of a thousand and one news broadcasts, documentaries, and newspaper articles. But this is worth dwelling on at some length because the Rohingya genocide is one of the most egregious human rights violations that can be directly linked to social media. As a case study, it also powerfully illustrates social media's ability to fuel and channel our worst impulses while suffocating the better angels of our nature, diverting us from nobler ends. To sum up in a riskily pithy form: social media is very good at crowdsourcing destroyers, and very bad at organizing builders.

***

Why is it this way? The answer is twofold. Firstly, once again, individualism. Riling up a single person to commit a hate crime furthers misery in the world, while encouraging an individual to, say, donate money to a homeless man on the street doesn't truly address the system that made him homeless, it merely salves an individual's pain. The latter action is, of course, virtuous and should be done. But awful individual actions tend to have a terroristic effect that cannot easily be balanced out by the dispensing of small blessings. Further, it is easy to perform literal crowdsourcing with social media — summoning a crowd to a location, say — but what comes next is, invariably, chaotic. Getting that crowd to build a new type of society, however earnest they may be, is extraordinarily challenging and frequently beyond the limited power of online platforms. But making a lot of people angry and turning them loose, in, say, a target-rich ethnic enclave is well within the scope.

Secondly, there is the issue of *power*. So much prejudice is often congenial with the aims of governments and elites; the genocide against the Rohingya was a culmination of long-standing policy aims held by several Burmese governments, including its junta. Trans people are proving to be useful scapegoats for the British government as it seeks to distract attention from its myriad policy failures, and a bogeyman for Republicans eager to find some "cultural" issue to rally their own voters with. These are only the most obvious examples. University of Washington communications scholar Katy Pearce published a study in 2015 entitled "Democratizing Kompromat: The Affordances of Social Media for State-Sponsored Harassment," about how the authoritarian government of Azerbaijan used social media campaigns to slander and silence critics.[23]

There's a comforting myth that circulated widely throughout the last decade in which social media allows for progressive revolutionary movements. As Greenwood notes, by the late aughts, "the Arab Spring, and the way in which its fearless millennial-aged leaders had organized on social media platforms that their authoritarian over-lords understood poorly, had ushered in a wave of global optimism" about Twitter and Facebook. That zeitgeist is, to some extent, still with us; see, for instance, the hope that surrounded the 2020 Black Lives Matter protests. But the critical part of that quote is the "understood poorly" bit.

If that was true in the late aughts, it's definitely not true today. And it was barely even true in the early 2010s, as Pearce's research demonstrates. The Azerbaijani government knew how to leverage Facebook memes well enough to dismiss and ridicule the opposition with astroturfing campaigns, or how to destroy an investigative journalist's life by releasing revenge pornography of her online. Meanwhile, the far right is as networked as the rest of us.

As with the example of guns discussed earlier, the tool's potential is dramatically amplified by its connection to legacy power structures. If the state or some other powerful institution is functionally on your side, then your online crowdsourcing can have very deleterious effects indeed. It's what has made the current wave of transphobia so dangerous, because it feeds a vicious cycle that many *lawmakers* are now seeking to perpetuate, even as they and the online agitators who campaign for them whip up mobs that can hurt or kill targeted individuals. When your harassment is backed by the full faith and credit of an actual state, with real guns, *then* social media gains a little bit more power to actually change things — if only for the worse.

This individualism-plus-power formula is at the heart of social media's greatest criminal hits, whether it's American fascists directing hate at a trans woman TikTokker or queer primary school teacher, or Indian fascists driving violent threats at a journalist who's reported critically on Narendra Modi's government, or people ratcheting each other up to go out and kill or rape an immigrant, a refugee, a member of some despised minority — whether it's the Rohingya in Burma, or Nigerians in South Africa, or a trans woman in the UK. Social media's great at that, and that dynamic is what has changed the world for the *worse*. Unfortunately, the same tools only permit us a particularly narrow kind of revenge. They do not help us achieve our loftier goals, nor make us any safer.

I need to quote Greenwood one more time, because I can't better their skeet about Twitter-esque platforms:

> Yes, you CAN participate in thrilling global discourse, but every time you post on Twitter, you roll dice to determine if THIS is the one that leads to strangers threatening to boil your family members for the next 5 years.

We take that risk for the sake of pleasure, yes, but we also take the risk to reap other individual rewards — to our careers, for instance. It's always a dice roll: Will I do some amazing networking that'll boost my income? Get crowdfund subscribers? Or death threats? In each case, the outcomes are resolutely individual. But because we're surrounded by a crowd of digital ghosts, it *feels* collective.

***

In the end, what draws us to social media is: 1) the ceaseless allure of catharsis, like Jay Gatsby's green light, bewitching us across the Long Island Sound, and 2) the vain hope that at the end of all our extravagant exertions, we'll have changed something meaningful in the world.

One is a mirage of an oasis, the other as real as a line of cocaine. Unfortunately, neither is the one we'd hope it is. Social media, as a fundamentally individualistic force, offers us catharsis. That's why Bluesky has ended up being an Ark of the Dramas for Twitter, because we can't easily let go of the quick hit of emotional expiation that platforms like this provide.

It's too easy to use these platforms as catharsis. In a world where mental health care remains a luxury and where other outlets for creative expression are increasingly closed off, posting remains a democratic art, for now. And yet, it is killing us at the same time, sapping the energy from progressive movements or swallowing them whole in boreholes of internet drama. It's Potemkin politics, mistaking personal soothing for political change.

There's little unique about Bluesky in this respect. After all, the most devilish trick pulled by these platforms was convincing us that our posts were praxis. Time and again, we found ourselves deluded into spending useful time and energy on what was little more than entertainment.

To give you a sense of how far this delusion could go, consider an example:

> **Ben Collins**
> **@bencollins@bsky.social**
> We had a good ten years where a bunch of nobodies like us could report on power centers and structural inequality and abuses of power and citizens from government, employers and their surrogates. The end of Twitter as that vehicle was the end of that, which was obviously the point.
> **Aug 2, 2023 at 3:11 pm 76 reposts 315 likes**
>
> |
> **Ben Collins**
> **bencollins@bsky.social**
> The people who really needed to consolidate power as workers started to defend themselves more got the world's biggest gift when Elon bought and desecrated the decade's most successful complaint hotline
> **20 reposts 116 likes**
>
> |
> **Luanne Platter**
> **@luanneplatter.bsky.social**
> I considered it my civil right... nay my civic duty... to call Ted Cruz a dickhead *directly* as often as was appropriate
> And I'm quite sure he saw some of those tweets
> **0 reposts 1 like**

This exchange on Bluesky is worth tens of thousands of words. Collins here extols the virtues of Twitter as a kind of civic platform that could rally the masses against the powerful. A tool so effective, it took a conspiracy of billionaires to run it into the ground, saving them from the mortal threat of our callout tweets. But the fact that he likens it to a "complaint hotline," one of the most quintessentially capitalist tools for the diffusion of anger, hints at the deeper problem.

And then, as if on cue, along comes a woman who likens writing mean tweets to Ted Cruz to civic duty, hoping that he saw some of them. There's hardly a better refutation of the idea that we all took Twitter much too seriously. *That* sort of thing — calling Ted Cruz a dickhead — was *all* that the platform was for. Not that it isn't a mitzvah, of course. May Ted Cruz be buried in cries of "Dickhead!" for all the rest of his undoubtedly miserable days. But we can't mistake this shouting for activism. More precisely, we can't mistake it for *social change*.

What it *is*, is precisely the thing social media is best at facilitating: individual catharsis. People like Collins needed to ennoble this because we needed to pretend it all meant something, that it had shaken the world to its very core in some fundamentally *productive* way. It didn't. And the pretending is costing us quite a lot.

***

During the bleakest days of the 2020 George Floyd protests — protests where two of the women I love most in this world were out putting their bodies on the line, day after day, night after night — I came to realize that even the most conservative appraisals of social media as a force for good in the world were not nearly pessimistic enough. As with past protest movements around the world — the Colour Revolutions, the Arab Spring, Hong Kong's democracy movement — the BLM protests were credited to social media, for spreading images quickly, puncturing official narratives, facilitating sousveillance, and, that old standby, "amplifying marginalized voices."

But as the protests ground themselves against the concrete barriers of the state, a funny thing began to happen. More and more organizing was migrating *off*-platform, with growing suspicion of anyone still trying to organize on open social media. We had, inevitably, reached the life cycle stage of protest movements where paranoia about cop infiltrators set in — fuelled by the simple reality of state-sponsored snitch operations like COINTELPRO in our history.

And yet, at the same time, I noticed factions of protesters begin to turn on each other and feud ever more openly on social media. One group was, broadly, seen as more "liberal," the other as more "radical," though this convenient, and somewhat inaccurate, dichotomy reifies what Twitter's illimitable bullshit was doing to these people. Each accused the other of being informants, or of otherwise aiding the police. Allegations flew thick and fast — some legitimate, some not, *all* occluding ongoing, necessary work and sapping momentum. It fed the alreadyinevitable paranoia.

Were there cops, masquerading as protesters, fomenting Twitter drama to divide them? Maybe! But even if not, the equal inevitability of Twitter drama being blown up into the Brobdingnagian politics of the end times ensured that the truth of that question never mattered. People were tearing each other down with suspicion, without any evident need for police intervention. While police informants and infiltrators are a real and ongoing threat to radical activism, ask yourself how much we *really* need their help to eat each other alive online. We're plenty capable of this on our own. (To say nothing of the fact that no one ever got rich betting on the wit or cunning of your average cop.)

The end result was that, far from being a magical secret sauce for radical protest, as Twitter's hagiographers would have us believe, the place became a liability.

I distinctly remember the "radical" wing of Seattle's protest movement holding an information session in a park one day. A perfectly reasonable-sounding woman wondered if — because of the smoke settling over the city in its now worryingly regular wildfire season — it would be possible for people to listen to a livestream of it. No, came the reply. Are you insane? No recordings, nothing identifiable, lest the police identify leaders, or just anyone to harass, regardless of their importance to the movement. Recordings help the cops.

This was, to a large extent, *true*. There were good reasons to not create endlessly reproducible media of this meeting. And yet here it was: the very link that social media was *supposed* to facilitate for activists was being severed. A normie, eager to learn more, trying to leverage the awe-inspiring power of social media to connect to a cause larger than herself... turned away and shouted at because no, actually, social media *was not a good place to do this*.

A combination of 1) legitimate fear, 2) the obvious panopticism of open platforms, where anyone, including the state, could be watching and listening, and 3) the paranoia engendered by social media beefs being given earth-shattering importance by the political context outside, came together to ensure that Twitter's supposedly mightiest purpose was all but neutered.

***

In his recent book *If We Burn*, the veteran foreign correspondent Vincent Bevins tried to explain why these sorts of movements keep failing and why the past decade of social-media-fired protest has left us with what he terms a "missing revolution."

He partially blames the platforms, even saying of journalists like himself that it was "a real problem that we are drawn so powerfully to the production of whatever will go viral on social media."[24] But these protests — in their anarchic, horizontalist, leaderless form — are also a reflection of social media itself. Instead of re-creating our activism on Twitter, we re-create Twitter in our activism.

This in turn, Bevins argues, owes itself to the "End of History" exuberance of the end of the Cold War, the (supposedly post-) ideological assumptions of the new order that emerged from the rubble of the Berlin Wall — a world where individual choice was all that mattered, and old, collective ideologies and institutions were no longer as important as they once were.

Bevins quotes an Italian sociologist, Paolo Gerbaudo, who studied and participated in many protests, who wrote, "At the end of the day, horizontalism is a reflection of individualism." Bevins is even more scathing: "A generation of individuals raised to view everything as if it were a business enterprise was de-radicalised, came to view this global order as 'natural,' and became unable to imagine what it takes to carry out a true revolution."[25]

I'm not sure I would go that far. But it's a hard argument to resist, not least because I find myself surrounded online by people who identify with the most left-wing of ideologies yet also remain lost to the consumerist discourse of platforms, privileging their emotions and personal moral purity above more tangible considerations — which is also more likely to win them the currency of attention.

When, at last, that person is summoned to the street, they take this social media-ready mindset with them. With disastrous results. And, as with the 2020 protests, social media often made it easier for the state to exact revenge against those who dared to defy it — however ineffectually.

If meaningful organizing that protected activists could not take place on Twitter, then what was it really *for*? There were still superficial levels of organizing that could take place. But even that may start to fade as new imperatives come to dominate our consolidated social media landscape.

It's worth noting that one of Twitter's most credible successors, Meta's Threads app, is now dispensing with even the pretence of supporting social movements. As this book was about to head to press, Meta announced that it would stop recommending "political content" to users on Instagram and Threads. How is this defined?

Meta's original blog post described it as "potentially related to things like laws, elections, or social topics." And what the hell are "social topics"? Am I a social topic? Potentially. The *Washington Post*'s Will Oremus asked a Meta spokeswoman for clarification. "Social topics can include content that identifies a problem that impacts people and is caused by the action or inaction of others, which can include issues like international relations or crime," she said. Such topics are not banned, of course, but discoverability will likely reach a new low. Meta clearly wants to get out of the game of appearing to be involved in politics. Like it or not, the choice of whether or not to log off if you want to change the world for the better is being made for you — either by Musk ceaselessly imposing his reactionary politics on what's left of Twitter's moderation, or by Threads imposing a brand-friendly meaninglessness on its successor platform. We are a long, long way from the halcyon days of early Twitter, when the company seemed eager to encourage the nobler mass movements of the world.

Even under these new conditions, social media will remain good at summoning lots of warm bodies to a particular location — whether for a protest against police violence, a McDonald's media crossover promotion of a unique sauce flavour, or an influencer claiming to give away free video game consoles. But it remains quite terrible at helping people decide *what comes next.*

Deliberation about next steps, how to capitalize on all those warm bodies, how to build and sustain momentum, descends rapidly into the wrecking and splintering that have always plagued the political left.[26] It just happens at lightspeed now, facilitated by the way social media encourages us to ennoble every beef with our loftiest ideals, no matter how personal or trivial.

It's "the personal is political" as the curling of a monkey's paw finger.

***

I find myself haunted by an exchange on Twitter that epitomizes Terminal Poster's Madness:

Best of Dying Twiter
@bestofdyingtwit
we have no choice but to stan 🐱
order taylor's book here for allll the stalker ex gf vibes: a.co/d/bk3f6wk

> **Ian Miles Cheong** ☑️
> **@stilgray**
> Taylor Lorenz uses X more than she uses Zuck's knockoff platform, where she endlessly posts about Elon Musk and how X is on the brink of collapse. This woman is obsessed.
>
>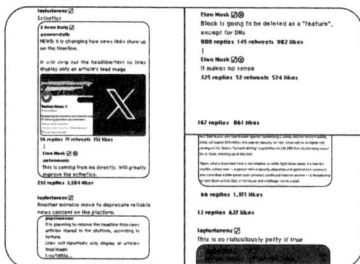
>
> **136 replies 120 retweets 1,569 likes**
>
> |
> **Elon Musk** ☑️ ⊗
> **@elonmusk**
> Stalker ex gf vibes
> **251 replies 138 retweets 2,228 likes**
>
> |
> **TaylorLorenz.substack.com**
> **@TaylorLorenz**
> Elon if you want to learn what happens when a silicone valley CEO mismanages and alienates the biggest creators on their platform, pre-order my new book EXTREMELY ONLINE!!

This is like that famous *Manchester Evening News* photo of New Year's Eve drunks laid out on the pavement — a blitzed man languidly reaching for his pint as he lazes in the middle of the street, a car right behind him, another man fighting with police while a woman angrily beckons. It's a Renaissance painting of imperial post-death. That's what the above screenshot is.

Like the photo, it has *everything*: one of the worst people on Twitter[27] trying to dunk on a tech reporter and calling her obsessed for writing about an important platform; Elon Musk once again dubbing any woman who exists within a thousand miles of him a stalker ex-girlfriend with unnervingly wistful vibes; and the reporter herself gleefully leaping on it all to deliver a hackneyed advert for a book to which she gave a shockingly un-self-aware title, engaged in her brand-burnishing clout-chasing. All framed by some account quote-tweeting a screenshot of all of this with a "yass kween" exhortation because she *totally owned* Musk.

What good is being done in this exchange? What, precisely, has Lorenz accomplished here beyond scoring a dunk that might net her a few (literally, a few) more book sales? Well, she added her clout to the platform she rightly criticizes, fuelling it, and fuelling Elon Musk's sense of importance as well as Ian Miles Cheong's inaccurate belief that he has the right to speak to anyone. Beyond that, nothing virtuous occurred here. This is not a place of honour; nothing valued is here.

The obsessiveness demonstrated by all parties is abundantly clear, and it's what keeps the fires burning. That eager willingness to dance with the demons of virality and micro-fame, to keep posting despite its toxic uselessness, is the habit we all have to break.

The thing that keeps me up at night is that we seem to only be able to do truly terrible things with Terminally Online behaviour; it's exceedingly rare that we can use it for good. Through her commitment to posting, Lorenz merely props up the platform and amplifies the worst people. By continuing to be on Twitter, she is lending the site her clout and credibility as a *Washington Post* journalist. For what? No, really, for *what*?

Ask yourself: Do you really need to add your cellular mass to this tumour? Is this *really* what you want to be a part of?

***

And here I have to catch myself because, of course, there *is* something here I want to be part of. As I said at the beginning of this chapter, it's the frivolity. Bluesky, the social media site I currently continue to be on, offers a good example, appropriately summarized by a meme of its own: the oft-repeated claim that "Bluesky is for the dolls."

Dolls (just in case you aren't one) is slang for transgender women.[28] What this meme asserts is that Bluesky is, can be, or must be made to be a safe haven for trans people; a place where we can flee from the depredations of a Twitter owned by a man who made his hatred of trans people an overriding policy objective. A Bluesky that's for the dolls is one where we can be ourselves openly and freely, where we can meme, flirt, grieve, joke, shitpost, flash our tits and our girlcocks (well, not me, I'm not brave enough), and generally do incredibly absurd and Extremely Online things at each other — and at our friends and allies of all stripes. There's a beautiful efflorescence on Bluesky of trans women and trans femmes being out, proud, discursive, lewd, funny, nerdy, and not infrequently uplifting.

Every time I looked for Bluesky nonsense to use as an example of some awful phenomenon, the Bluesky dolls always restored some of my hope for the place. Even as I know that Bluesky will likely never gain the pole star position Twitter once occupied in the firmament of the cultural mainstream, I realize that's for the best, and that the lack of limelight will allow these dolls — and other queers and trans folks — to flourish, accosted by fewer Nazis, TERFs, and chuds.

Bluesky right now is a place where one of the most prominent trans shitposters — whom I shall embarrass my naming her as Kairi, Estrogen Empress (incidentally, she's also the volunteer mute-list maintainer I mentioned earlier) — can go viral for posting about the purchase of a sundress for the object of her desire, Bennie, for the purposes of the "railing" that is (according to the meme) paradigmatically occasioned by the wearing of such garments. It's a place where their trans romance can charm dozens, even hundreds, of people at once, blossoming *entirely* because of the platform, without which they would never have met.

Kairi takes this quality of Bluesky rather seriously. She recently skeeted

> Trans women being down bad for each other is the literal foundation of this little corner of the website and I will fight like hell to make sure it keeps happening

I was feeling sentimental, so I skeeted in reply

> So say we all.

If I'd been feeling a touch spiritual as well, I might have said instead, *So mote it be.* How else apart from on the internet can trans people, a micro-minority if ever there was one, meet each other at all?

***

Throughout this book, I've dwelt at length on examples involving transgender people — examples both good and bad. You might have wondered why I seem so very interested in this group. If so, perhaps you've drawn one obvious conclusion: I'm a transsexual woman myself and, like so many other ladies of letters before me, I am cursed to write what I know.

Certainly, online trans community is something I do know. But I want to make a bolder claim than that. The truth is that there is no history of the internet that can be adequately told without telling the story of what it did for trans people.

Regardless of what British newspapers might have us believe, we are and remain a tiny percentage of the population. Our numbers are small — at most peeking just over 1 percent of the population. We don't stumble onto each other easily out in the physical world.

I remain transfixed by tales of trans women from the mid-twentieth century who acted as literal post offices for their fellows. These rare people — almost always women — became prominent in national media and then absorbed the inevitable letters from fellow-travellers from all over. The celebrity in question would act as a router, linking people with one another by request. It was painstaking, manual, gut-wrenching, and vital. Such one-woman post offices probably saved lives, connecting people who might otherwise have had no chance whatsoever of meeting anyone like them.

And then, in the 1990s, that function was suddenly automated. Websites proliferated, blogs became the communiqué *du jour*, and suddenly transness was *networked*. Without any manual intervention whatsoever, that dispersed 1 percent of the world could find each other.

That, in many ways, is the miracle of the internet *for us all*. For people who loved to knit, or who enjoyed model trains, or Dungeons & Dragons, or Lego, or banana slugs, or Romanian stamps, it became possible to find people just like you — however rare you were. Open social media made it even easier. It knocked down the barriers between once-monadic websites and blogs. Suddenly everyone could talk to everyone, and then the most esoteric hobbies and lifestyles and identities could network all the more easily.

If, online, ontogeny really is phylogeny, then the birth of a new, successful networking platform will always be accompanied by some micro-minority finding and reconstituting itself there. The virtuous version of this phenomenon very often takes the form of transgender people. And it does so not by accident, but because it's rare that we find ourselves in large numbers elsewhere.

However, there is also a fiendish beneficiary of this crowdsourcing: Nazis. It's not a coincidence that the online Nazi hub Stormfront, frequented by the likes of terrorist Anders Breivik, has been around since the very earliest days of the modern internet. The internet writ large, social media most particularly, draws together the smallest of small minorities who might not otherwise be able to find each other. For good and for ill. In many ways, that's the story of the so-called Information Age.

***

I am a product of the virtuous side of that dynamic. I first visited TSRoadmap.com back in 2007, pretending that I'd come there purely on behalf of a friend who wanted to transition. Reading just that one website was something like the ending of *2001: A Space Odyssey*, a psychedelic shattering of everything I thought I knew, culminating in rebirth. There is a very real degree to which I owe my entire life — a life worth living — to being online.

I don't want to steal that away from someone else, from some young child in Ron DeSantis's Florida who may find some happy reflection of the person they want to be, a vision of a community they can thrive in, somewhere on social media. When I look at Bluesky — Ark of the Dramas though it may sometimes be — I see something that could look like paradise to the lost. Witty, charming, beautiful trans people and non-binary folks, laughing, joking, being proud, being flirty, being snarky, giving each other the most loving shit — my Goddess, the things I could say, the references I could make that only ten people would get.

Would you believe me if I told you someone named Katie Tightpussy who reviewed movies and was fake-cancelled by her friends ten times before noon every day as a sort of ritual was a real woman who walked this earth? Or walked this internet, at least.

It's a silly scene. But it's one that some small sliver of the population might really want to be a part of. If the matte painting I just brushed up there doesn't speak to you, consider your own esoteric interests or identities and how the internet connected you to people who didn't think you were irredeemable. Hell, social media made Dungeons & Dragons mainstream.

I deny none of this, and I'm not trying to take it away from any of you. I'd have to take away my entire *career*, the very life I've built. But it is on that basis, with the richness of that experience, that I am still asking you to log off — at least provisionally. If you log off, at least for a little while, you'll be able to think very critically about what that networking *actually* is. Because, for all its real results, it remains individualistic.

It's powerful. Powerful enough to save your life. But is it politics? It may be a precondition of politics — you can't politick if you're not alive — but it's not the thing itself. If trans community is emblematic of the potential of social media for networking micro-minorities through passive crowdsourcing — one of its chief affordances — it is also a prime example of that crowdsourcing's limits. Social media helps us transition, but it doesn't necessarily help us organize.

There are more trans people coming out, and more of us talking to one another, than ever before, and that has had salubrious downstream effects. But have we really been able to bring about a polity that values transgender rights and dignity as axiomatic? The record is mixed, to say the least. If we have made any progress to that end, it has not been because of social media, but because of the patient and agonizing political work that happens in courts and legislatures, on the streets and in our non-profits — organizations like the legal aid society I once volunteered for, the Sylvia Rivera Law Project.

The virtues of "awareness" and 'visibility," by contrast, are few and compromised.* But visibility and awareness are all that social media can provide in abundance. For something more substantial, one needs to get away from the cavalcades of callouts and Main Characters and other assorted forms of illusory justice *du jour*.

None of this ought to take away from Bluesky being, most assuredly, *for the dolls* — if that means a place for, say, trans women to find each other and share joy, japes, and sluttiness. These insights, far from being contradictory, are, in reality, complementary. Social media does politics poorly; it facilitates the railing of people in sundresses quite well. We don't need to stop the latter to acknowledge the former.

Then, when we do log off, it can be to do the hard, patient work of activism. This can be time spent volunteering, time spent building a real organization, time spent campaigning and petitioning, time spent getting to know your neighbours or finding your fellow-travellers where you actually live.[29] And then logging on to, say, Nightsky to be down bad for someone ten time zones away.

....

* See: *Trap Door: Trans Cultural Production and the Politics of Visibility*, eds. Tourmaline, Eric A. Stanley, and Joshua Burton.

Conclusion:
Log Off!

To Log Off is semiotically complex. It doesn't necessarily mean "log off forever, and never touch a computer again, you canned ham of a man" (although it *can* if you're talking to Nate Silver). Usually, it just means "step away for a bit." It means "let go for a while." It means "touch grass," as the popular parlance of our time would have it. (I'd have called this book *Touch Grass*, but I should leave that for an intrepid weed journalist.) Obviously, I can't ask you to log off entirely. I can't even manage it myself. I don't even want to manage it myself. After all, when it is used for frivolity and personal sociality, social media can be wonderful. But when we use the internet for serious purposes, we must do so with intent and not pretend that shouting into the void is activism.

We need to remember that the leadership of social media platforms don't have our best interests at heart either. Even if they're trying — and they're usually not. Whether it's TikTok, Tumblr, Bluesky, or some other open platform, the ultimate point is to keep us there, making the place our one-stop shop for all our social needs.

When Elon Musk farts out another idea for how to make Twitter an "everything app," he's simply saying the quiet part out loud. Their aspirations are to make their sites as essential as possible to our lives, for work, play, finances, education, and entertainment, with thousands of subheadings beneath each.

You know by now I'm not a believer in individualized solutions to collective problems, but the power we have, in the face of this acquisitive drive, is the power to walk. To log off is to deprive the social media engines of fuel. We are the oxygen for every conflagration, every bit of drama that we think is so terribly important in the moment. Such episodes are immediately lost to history but rob *us* of something we can never get back. In exchange for a drop of catharsis, we lose a pint of lifeblood that could instead be spent on real work in the world outside.

Queer and trans people are caught in an especial bind here, because social media platforms are often the only place some of us can find community worth having. Perhaps you live in a small town in a conservative area, or perhaps you've moved to a new city and left your old community behind. But I think it's worth remembering that the fleeting, Potemkin "community" we see on social media is a very recent invention, and was never anyone's experience of community before the mid-1990s.

We can still use the vast power of the internet to network and maintain connections: instant messaging services, IMs, Discord or Slack servers, private forums, and more. And while Discord can incubate drama, frankly the worst of it tends to come from Discord screenshots being posted on more open platforms. (If I had a dime for every time Bluesky drama originated from Discord chatrooms, I'd be able to buy the place and ban everyone.) As challenging as it can be to moderate an active Discord server, it's still easier than trying to corral the egos of millions of people at once. We can stay in touch with loved ones while minimizing damage to our psyches. And when something *does* go wrong, private platforms contain the problem and make it harder to spiral.

It was not uncommon for civic activists, tired of waiting for their city or town councils to make their local streets safer, to pour the asphalt and make their own speed bumps to slow down cars. And then there were the disability activists who used sledgehammers to bust up sidewalk curbs so that their cities could replace them with curb cuts for wheelchairs.

We need to do the same with the infrastructure of the internet, adding the friction we need to keep ourselves healthy, putting in our own speed bumps and curb cuts. We cannot wait for Big Tech to build it; their profits depend on them *not*. Friction makes it *harder* for the stuff of our private lives to travel when we don't want it to, as well as protecting us from everyone else's distracting bullshit. It's not ideal, it won't fix Big Tech's myriad crises nor save us all from them. But we can save ourselves and those we love—and we most definitely should.

***

Much existing criticism of social media seeks either to castigate the internet as a whole or to suggest that some ideal version of it can be achieved, usually with sufficiently aggressive content moderation. But social media itself, the specific instantness of the internet that promises everyone-to-everyone communication at all hours, is the core of the problem.

People will call you a Luddite (pejorative) if you suggest this, arguing that every major technological leap forward was accompanied by inane calls to rewind the clock. But social media is not, itself, the giant step for humankind. Social media represents a very particular *use* of the larger technological advance that enables it.

If we're going to form an analogy to what revolutionized the world in eras past, let's try railroads. The revolution that overthrew the British in India and Pakistan was fomented by the railways, which allowed ideas *and people* to spread with all the electric vibrations of the telegraph lines that paralleled the rails. The claim that apologists for social media often make is essentially that it is, or can become, the *world's* Indian Railways. But it isn't. The proper analogy here is the internet itself:

global networking and instant communication across infinitely porous borders. *That* enables much. But harping on social media as some threshold whence we may never return is like fixating on the ostentatiously hostile design of a particular train station as essential to the future of civilization. It's an experiment, and it failed.

We've been buried under a decade and more's worth of "social media-driven" revolutions that fell well short of their ambitions. How Colour Revolutions ran aground, how Occupy Wall Street ultimately fizzled, how various other protest movements fell far short of what they aspired to. At what point will we admit that social media is far from a secret ingredient for lasting change?

Much of the hope that social media offers is the same hope that former Meta COO Sheryl Sandberg held out to women at the end of *Lean In*'s introduction: "We can reignite the revolution by internalizing the revolution. The shift to a more equal world will happen person by person." This, in the end, is the promise of platforms that people like Sandberg helped build. Individualism, neatly fitted with capitalist goals. Change yourself, change the world.

It's a recipe for enthroning one's base desires or misunderstood needs above the needs of a community. In the end, that isn't hope. That's the *death* of hope. We are not ready—nor should we ever be ready—to channel our best aspirations through these platforms that are designed to melt them into the air of profit.

What I can hope is that we all, together, start to think differently about social media as a *tool* designed to do specific things — things that are rarely in line with our more aspirational goals. We must match our goals with the affordances of the platforms. Signal's encryption is ideal for sensitive conversations. Microblogging platforms can advertise a rally. Discord can host intimate dialogues. I hope that we will adapt our strategies to our purposes. Or, to put it less clinically, that we can use social media for what it's best at and log the fuck off for the rest of the time.

But above all, all the activism we do online *must* be tethered firmly to the physical world. And the more intentional we are about how we use social media, the more we'll ensure that social media doesn't use *us*.

***

Hannah Arendt's vision of politics — like so much of her philosophy — is shrouded in sometimes dense prose, but it amounts to a useful way of thinking about these issues. Real politics, for her, begins from *action*, which means using one's fundamental freedom to do or become something new:

> The fact that man is capable of action means that the unexpected can be expected from him, that he is able to perform what is infinitely improbable. And this again is possible

only because each man is unique, so that with each birth something uniquely new comes into the world.[30]

What is new, she says, "therefore always appears in the guise of a miracle." Politics is the vehicle for those miracles.

But Arendtian politics has another quality: it is pluralistic. We are not great lords of history heroically moving the whole of the world on some Archimedean lever; we are, in the end, one person among many. And while each of us represents a natal miracle of infinite possibility, we can only realize *political* aims by acting in concert.

Social media seemed to offer a way of nearly automating the latter, crowdsourcing us with little to no conscious input from ourselves. But in the process of automating that, we lose the ability to weave miracles on most days. The automation inherently robs us of *intentional* communities. Worse yet, by encouraging our most self-centred instincts, by making us too intimately concerned with salving our emotions and private virtue, social media in its current form has made pluralism *harder* for us to achieve.

When we tear each other apart over the narcissism of small differences — a plague on activism that long predates social media but has been dramatically accelerated by it — we are denying ourselves the ability to *actually* do politics, to convert our actions into the miracle of change. We endlessly recycle uselessly discursive[31] nonsense in a strained bid to make ourselves feel momentarily better, momentarily more certain, momentarily less alone; and, in the process, instead of building a lasting political community, the kind of entity that could create change, we lose it all in a haze of recriminations.

Instead, we could be *out there*, making miracles.

Acknowledgements

The author of a book is only the most obvious member of a small community that comes together to assemble this particular set of ideas in its particular place and time. This is my first solo-authored non-fiction book and it represents the culmination of a lifelong aspiration, one that I owe to my own little community of friends, allies, influencers, lovers, and more.

It is customary to leave one's loved ones for last in these things, but I'm sure that my colleagues will forgive me if I put the light of my life first. I couldn't have done this without my partner-for-life, Rachel K. Zall, poetess, photographer, smut-peddler, and a woman who has been an intellectual partner in the truest sense of the word. Any errors in this text are my own, but the ideas herein are the product of a decade of conversations that one has with someone they love. The book you hold in your hands is the child of so many conversations between us that took place all over the world. I'd also like to thank her for something else: putting up with me when I'd giggle in bed in the middle of the night, only for her to patiently ask me, "are you thinking about memes again?"

There is also another interlocutor whom I must thank right up front: Casey Plett, one of the two illustrious editors of this text. Casey and I have a friendship that I can only characterize as an endless, open, honest conversation. Her careful eye—at once scrutinising and compassionate—has made this book infinitely better than it might otherwise have been.

Cat Fitzpatrick also brought an inimitable editorial flourish to this book. Taken together, these two women have given me the most fruitful editorial experience I've ever had, and I've benefitted in no small measure from great editors in the past.

I must also spare a quick thank you to the graphic designer, Zack Bokhur, for his endless patience with my nitpicking about the cover.

I'd also like to thank my cunning fox of a girlfriend Ellen Leal for her comments on earlier drafts, and for her bottomless faith in me. Claire, I thank you for the endless conversations—and for the night you pulled me in for a kiss in the cloak where you keep your daggers. Many thanks, meanwhile, are owed Faine Greenwood for their comments on a near final-draft of this book and for bequeathing us Alf-Hog on Bluesky (if you know, you know).

Other Bluesky posters like Kairi, Estrogen Empress; Sage; Katie Tightpussy; Ride on the Magic Skeetbus; Cartoon Dog GF (Jazz); Uncut Femmes;

Chelsea Bridge; Micah; Edith Charles; Lo Scoiattalo; Ripperoni; Tall F. Pompkins (Hattie); Stovey, and many, many more provided me with provocations, hours of laughter, sobriety, insight, and a reminder that for all my accumulated bitterness from a decade of microblogging, the concept still has The Juice.

Their influence on this text is less tangible, but I assure you that without them it would've been more cynical. To them is owed the very idea behind me naming the penultimate chapter "Bluesky is for the Dolls" and the thin filament of faith I have in Bluesky's promise to produce a new, better generation of microblogging. While I very much doubt this book will please the people who *run* Bluesky, it is, nevertheless, a love letter to it.

Thanks also to my IRL friends and lovers: Dillon Trethewey for endless conversation and encouragement and the odd drink; Katie Kita, an old friend without parallel; my beloved Elizabeth Goodman for her moral compass and a sense of virtue; Anna Elisabeth Lavender for always being able to talk shop with precision, snark, and precise snark; Emily Lynch for the sincerest encouragement I can imagine; Kiva for reading and making me feel special; Rachel Jacqueline, for the way you call me 'doll' and for always listening; Sabriel, for being my Viking of the Prairies; Anastasia Schaadhardt for cuddles, helping me figure out what the hell is going on with TikTok, and for always holding me in the light — when I returned to the idea of people earnestly trying to change the world with the tools at their disposal, it is her smiling face I frequently thought of.

I am enmeshed in an academic community which has nurtured me as a scholar, and bits and pieces of my analysis always belong to all of you in some small way. Thank you to Os Keyes, Florence Chee, Celia Pearce, Emma Westecott, T.L. Taylor, Anna Lauren Hoffmann, Mary Gray, Emily van der Nagel, Mahli-Ann Butt, Sarah Stang, Emma Vossen, Adrienne Shaw, Amanda Friz, Carole Palmer, Alex DiBranco, Ariella Schiff, Rosalind Petchesky, Pamela Stone, and many more besides.

On the journalism side, the people who have most nurtured me as a writer for popular audiences include the other greatest editors I've ever known: Laura Hudson, Kjerstin Johnson, Angela Chen, Jos Truitt, and Nikki Gloudeman. I also learned a lot from my fellow trans journalists, essayists, and polemicists: Jude Ellison S. Doyle, Emily St. James, Katelyn Burns, and others.

A note of thanks must also be offered to Zorana, aka Lady Z, one of the coolest bartenders I've ever known, and who's slung me tea, mocktails, and vodka shots aplenty while I was writing large chunks of this text at her Gothy bar. But thanks are also due to Jason, Eden, Sarah, Jean, Kurt, Eddie, Ed, Riley, and Neah for their provision of libations and foodstuffs.

Finally, I must, of course, thank my parents. When I put a pen in my own hand, they didn't take it away. My father pulled a 1967 Encyclopedia

Britannica out of the trash to help educate me, and filled our house with books that I wanted to read — and learn from. My mother encouraged me as I wrote my first (extremely bad) "novel" on looseleaf paper, always urging me forward once I learned to use this mysterious thing called a word processor. They knew very little about education, much less its fruits, but they knew that it was *important*.

Writers write to be read, and we pray that what we write *deserves* to be read. To this day I always feel a certain sense of astonishment that anyone would care about my writing, and I feel tremendous gratitude every time I receive a complimentary email, social media share or post, or any other sign that what I wrote mattered to you. To *anyone* who reads me: thank you. It is the highest compliment a writer could receive.

To all the above, my heartfelt thanks for making this book possible. If I forgot anyone, my most sincere apologies, and my bottomless gratitude, for all you've given me.

Endnotes

1 For a truly excellent, ground-level analysis of this phenomenon, read Vincent Bevins, *If We Burn: The Mass Protest Decade and the Missing Revolution* (2023, Public Affairs).

2 A classic Matt Bors cartoon from *The Nib*. https://thenib.com/mister-gotcha/

3 https://www.theatlantic.com/technology/archive/2022/11/twitter-facebook-social-media-decline/672074/

4 https://www.technologyreview.com/2023/10/17/1081194/how-to-fix-the-internet-online-discourse/

5 Seriously, it's kind of a banger (also slightly offensive and such a remarkable relic of its time) https://www.youtube.com/watch?v=vcsS-SawHys8

6 For the sake of posterity, I will mention that this "debate" was mostly centred on the use of "trans-inclusive" language, including gender-neutral terms for experiences like pregnancy or breastfeeding. Inclusive language was rarely taken up publicly, though occasionally included in training materials for a small number of health care workers. On social media, however, these language debates were very prominent, and if someone — like, say, a *New York Times* columnist or once-beloved children's book author—spent far too much time on Twitter, then they, like a Chernobyl liquidator, would be exposed to many, many times the safe lifetime dose of radiation and mutate.
The prominence of these debates on social media vastly overstated the ability of trans people and their allies to reshape language or institutions; but for an obsessive who spends too much time on these platforms to begin with, subject to all the distorting effects of the Timeline, they might start to convince themselves that "'trans-in-

clusive language" was taking over every street corner in the Western world. Indeed, this is the way stochastic terrorists like Libs of TikTok surround their followers with an atmosphere made of confirmation bias, finding isolated examples from low-follow accounts and casting them as hegemonic. Add in some alliances with powerful entities and you have yourself a force that can change the destinies of countless innocent people. See the final chapter of this book for further explanation of this dynamic.

7 Because I hate myself, I looked it up for you. It reads as follows: "'People who menstruate.' I'm sure there used to be a word for those people. Someone help me out. Wumben? Wimpund? Woomud?" This tweet was her very-not-mad response to some newspaper article using the phrase "people who menstruate" in an attempt to respect the fact that some non-binary people and trans men do, in fact, have menstrual cycles.

8 https://www.newyorker.com/news/daily-comment/why-i-quit-elon-musks-twitter

9 https://slate.com/technology/2023/10/elon-musk-x-twitter-news-links-headlines-why.html

10 https://www.theguardian.com/technology/2023/jul/08/twitter-demise-journalists-eulogy-threads-app-elon-musk

11 *ibid.*

12 https://www.theverge.com/2022/11/11/23453236/twitter-eulogy-elon-musk

13 https://www.youtube.com/watch?v=62cPPSyoQkE

14 At the risk of bogging down this section, by the way, this quote is worth highlighting because, in his Substack, Yglesias buttresses the "very rapid increase" claim with an article from *Education Week* whose title—"Number of Trans Youth Is Twice as High as Previous Estimates, Study Finds" — appears to be the only bit of it he read. The reporter, Eesha Pendharkar, who likely didn't write the headline herself, observes the following:

While about 1.3 million adults identify as transgender based on survey results from the Centers for Disease Control's Behavior Risk Factor Surveillance System, that only accounts for 0.5 percent of the adult U.S. population. Previous estimates of the numbers of trans youth were extrapolated from that adult count... But in 2017, the CDC added a question about transgender identity to its Youth Risk Behavior Survey for high schoolers. Based on years of data from that survey and statistical models developed by Herman and others, the researchers found that among teenagers ages 13-17, 300,000 identify as transgender, which adds up to 1.4 percent of the nation's population within that age group.

I quote this in full because it illustrates that the "very rapid increase" is likely a statistical mirage. You're comparing a direct survey — the first of its kind — with a number that was divined as an extrapolation from a figure that measured an adult population. According to a breathless Reuters analysis of American insurance data, for instance, the number of children who used puberty blockers has gone up, yes, from 633 to 1,390, over the last six years. For reference, there are approximately 73.1 million people under the age of eighteen in the US, according to the 2020 census.

What does this have to do with this book? Well, consider how easy it is to lie about this on Twitter in a few characters, and look at how much verbiage I had to expend debunking it. I'll never, ever endorse threats against men like Yglesias; it's both morally empty and practically stupid. Equally, this shouldn't obscure the fact that men like him do a *lot* of harm with social media, even as they purport to criticize it.

15 See Emily St. James's excellent "How Twitter Can Ruin a Life" for more on this. St. James also suggests that Fall may have halted her transition: "As a trans woman early in transition, Fall had the option of retreating to the relative safety of her legal, masculine identity.

Katherine Cross

That's what she did, staying out of the limelight and growing ever more frustrated by what had happened to her. She bristles when I ask her in an email if she's stopped transitioning, but it's the only phrase I can think of to describe how the situation appears." https://www. vox.com/the-highlight/22543858/isabel-fall-attack-helicopter

16 "Never believe that anti-Semites are completely unaware of the absurdity of their replies. They know that their remarks are frivolous, open to challenge. But they are amusing themselves, for it is their adversary who is obliged to use words responsibly, since he believes in words. The anti-Semites have the right to play. They even like to play with discourse for, by giving ridiculous reasons, they discredit the seriousness of their interlocutors. They delight in acting in bad faith, since they seek not to persuade by sound argument but to intimidate and disconcert. If you press them too closely, they will abruptly fall silent, loftily indicating by some phrase that the time for argument is past." From *Anti-Semite and Jew* (1946).

17 Gibson, J. J. (1971). The senses considered as perceptual systems. *Journal of the British Society for Phenomenology*, 2(2), 104-105.

18 Evans, S. K., Pearce, K. E., Vitak, J., & Treem, J. W. (2017). Explicating Affordances: A Conceptual Framework for Understanding Affordances in Communication Research. *Journal of Computer-Mediated Communication*, 22(1), 35-52. https://doi.org/10.1111/jcc4.12180

19 Davis, J. L. (2020). *How Artifacts Afford: The Power and Politics of Everyday Things*. The MIT Press.

20 There are numerous examples I could have chosen from Bluesky to illustrate its Twitter-esque qualities, but the Poster's Strike was one of the choicest forms of weaponized sincerity I'd yet seen on the site. It grew out of the sex worker brouhaha that ensnared dril, along with credible allegations that Bluesky wasn't taking racism on the platform seriously enough—especially anti-Black racism. This stemmed, in part, from an incident where someone was able to create an account using the n-word as a username and it went undetected for weeks (though

231

there is some dispute about whether the user changed their username to the slur after being dormant for that whole time with a more innocuous username). In my own reporting at the time, I got unsatisfying answers from Bluesky when I asked about their Trust and Safety policy; they responded with vague platitudes but no specifics about future plans nor even the number of people working on T&S.

Anyway, the way some then-prominent Bluesky users responded was to threaten a "Posters' Strike," a new nadir of self-important social media usage borrowing the clothes of activism like a small child wearing their mother's business suit.

This 'strike" was supposed to represent a refusal to be funny, post lewds, or otherwise do anything likely to generate lots of engagement. It was disorganized and held together primarily through the glue stick of shaming—like the earlier episode mentioned where someone told off the Vagina Museum for making a post during the "strike."

Needless to say, nothing really happened here, though I can understand the temptation to think of something like this as potentially worthwhile activism. You see, in an earlier draft of this book, when I was writing the chapter urging people to quit Twitter, I used the phrase "you should withhold your labour." But posting is not labour. A strike works because the actual labour being withheld is essential for the operation of a collective entity — a factory, a bus network, a school, a store — and it cannot be easily replaced. But it also works because that labour is organized from the top down through a union, with infrastructure in place to administer the union and take care of striking workers who may go for long periods without pay. This is similar to why the famous Montgomery Bus Boycott worked; it was an organized effort with supportive infrastructure, including mass carpooling for the city's Black residents, to ensure they weren't too affected by the boycott.

But even if the "Poster's Strike" had been better organized, posting is not truly labour. The one exception to this might be sex workers, whose labour frequently requires some form of social media interaction — for advertising and building community and so on. But the strike, while it included them, was much broader and included non-sex-work lewds, humour, and shitposting. None of which could easily be described as "work." Finally, the strikers seemed to overestimate their numbers and their importance to the platform; there was never a meaningful response from Bluesky tied directly to the strike. They did, however, eventually and belatedly respond to the anger on the platform about anti-Black racism. See here for more: https://mashable.com/article/bluesky-racism-username-anti-blackness.

I suppose you can say the strike was part of that anger, but the primary effect of it was mostly to give certain prominent posters something new to scold people about rather than much in the way of material changes to the platform experience. Content was still constant, these people were still frequently posting—just advertising their "striking" more often than not—while many others continued in blissful ignorance of this supposed uprising.

At any rate, a search for the term *Poster's Strike* on Bluesky now merely brings up months' worth of jokes. It's now a meme describing a variant of Poster's Madness, taking oneself far too seriously online. An early variant read as follows: "im on poster's strike because im honestly rather tired of seeing the striking posters' strike posts." Which, you know, fair. Other jokes involve silly requests for things and jokingly threatening a strike, e.g., "Poster's strike until reply's are sorted by oppression!" And, of course, one of my favourites: "Wish I was here during the poster's strike . . . didn't realize something funny happened on this app for the first time ever."

The cycle is now firmly skewed towards irony and shitposting — because the greatest sin of the Poster's Strike was that it was too cringe. By which one means it involved caring too much; it was too earnest. So the site will have a good laugh about this, until the next thing comes along that makes everyone Serious Internet Activists for five minutes, after which no one will admit to having cared about whatever that was. The Aristocrats.

But hey, in the meantime, all of Bluesky's ironic mockery of the Poster's Strike is really funny.

21 Kissane's essay can be found here: https://erinkissane.com/meta-in-myanmar-part-i-the-setup

22 Greenwood's essay is also worth reading in full as a searching, personal reflection of a time that seems so far away now, but was practically yesterday: https://faineg.com/facebook-destroys-everything-part-1/

23 Pearce, K. E. (2015). Democratizing kompromat: The affordances of social media for state-sponsored harassment. *Information, Communication & Society*, 18(10), 1158-1174In the interest of full disclosure, Katy Pearce is a member of my graduate committees.

24 Bevins, V. (2023). If We Burn: The Mass Protest Decade and the Missing Revolution. Public Books. (p. 278).

25 *Ibid.* (p. 271).

26 A certain type of reader probably knew this cite was coming, but: Freeman, J. (1972). THE TYRANNY OF STRUCTURELESSNESS. *Berkeley Journal of Sociology*, 17, 151-164.

27 Ian Miles Cheong is a far-right social media influencer who had previously been trying to position himself as a liberal feminist during the GamerGate era of 2014-15. However, when that failed to win him the attention and praise he sought, he underwent the carcinogenesis of so many other disaffected "men of the left" angry with the excesses of SJWs (or the "wokes," as the latest bit of anti-language would term us). Now he spends his days looking for head pats from Elon Musk, as seen here. Happily for Cheong, despite Musk's enormous power and wealth, he's insecure enough to actually favour Cheong with attention.

28 I retain a bit of nostalgia for when we called ourselves "tall girls," which was especially aspirational for my five-foot-three-inch ass.

29 The idea of protest *alone* — even violent protest — as the most valorous or effective form of resistance is dramatically overstated, and the wreckage of the last decade makes the point. Social media promotes a kind of fetish for protest aesthetics and theatricality that leads to borderline brain-dead analyses of protest writ large. See, for instance, the many socialists who claimed that January 6, or the recent protests by right-wing French farmers, were some kind of genuine cry of the unheard.

A tweet by the leftist journal *Jacobin*, for instance, summarized one of their own articles by saying, "France's protesting farmers have broken the neoliberal framework in which the establishment wants to confine all political discussion about agriculture. That itself is a victory." Liberal analyst Jeremiah Johnson had it exactly right when he replied with this characterization: "*Jacobin* defending right-wing protestors who want cheaper fossil fuels and more handouts for land-owning farmers actually makes a ton of sense, once you realize most internet leftism is about the *~*vibes*~* of protest stunts, and French farmers do really killer protest stunts."

Logging off requires stepping back from this kind of Extremely Online cheerleading. In the absence of taking action ourselves, we're vulnerable to valorizing *anyone* who takes action, regardless of their motivations. Because, after all, "at least someone is doing *something*." Well. Why not you?

30 Arendt, H. (1958) *The Human Condition*. University of Chicago Press. (p. 178).

31 For all you Foucauldians out there, I do not mean "discourse" — i.e., productive discourse — in the sense Foucault meant it. I mean Discourse as in disc horse.

About LittlePuss Press

LittlePuss Press is a feminist press run by two trans women, Cat Fitzpatrick and Casey Plett.

We believe in printing on paper, intensive editing, and throwing lots of parties.

Typographical Note

The body of this text is set in Cormorant, a typeface designed by Christian Thalmann in 2015, inspired by the work of Claude Garamond (c.1510-1561). Unlike earlier typefaces inspired by Garamond, Cormorant specifically harnesses the high resolutions 21st-century technology affords both in print and on screen.

The quotations from microblogging platforms, together with chapter titles, running headers and so on, are set in Lo-Res, an original typeface designed by Zuzana Licko in 1985 . Unlike later digital typefaces, Lo-Res specifically capitalizes on the low resolutions afforded by 20th-century computer screens and printers.

Isn't progress wonderful?